Basketmaking

KAY JOHNSON

Basketmaking

B. T. BATSFORD LTD · LONDON

In loving memory of Jervis,
who gave me so much patient help and
encouragement.

First published 1991

Typeset by Lasertext Ltd, Stretford, Manchester
and printed in Great Britain by
Butler & Tanner, Frome, Somerset

Published by
B. T. Batsford Ltd
4 Fitzhardinge Street, London W1H 0AH

A catalogue record for this book is available from the British Library

ISBN 0 7134 6669 3

Contents

Acknowledgements

I am particularly indebted to Susan Colman for her help with the graphics, Bill and Felicity Crawforth and Louise Johnson for the drawings, Rev. Phillip Spence for the cartoons, Dave Kent for the cover photo and many of the others in the book.

I would like to thank members of the Basketmakers' Association and the many other friends who have helped and encouraged me, particularly Olivia Elton Barratt, Mary Butcher, Fred Rogers, Mary Connell and Joleen Gordon.

Introduction

I have written this book with the beginner in mind, although there are projects that the more advanced basketmaker may find new and challenging.

The text describes in detail the techniques and terminology used and there are over 100 diagrams and photographs to help. Each project uses the skills learned in the previous ones, so it is important for the beginner to start with the Rag Basket and work through.

Cane, imported from the Far East, is relatively inexpensive and can be purchased at most craft shops. It comes in about 15 different sizes, but in order to make things as simple as possible I have kept the number down to a minimum. The materials needed for each basket are clearly listed.

Each project teaches you how to make an attractive and useful basket. By following the simple instructions for colouring cane and including other materials: rush, willow, hedgerow, rags, etc., a unique touch can be added to each basket.

In the first project the basket is made on a wooden base so the beginner can concentrate on learning the basic weaves. Subsequently many baskets have instructions for making with both a wooden and a woven base, so that you can choose whichever method you prefer.

Experimentation is great fun and basketry is a very satisfying craft. I do hope that after working your way through this book you will have had many hours of enjoyment, either on your own or in a class, and that you will have gained a sound knowledge of basketmaking and its traditional vocabulary.

Tools and materials

MATERIALS

You can buy several different qualities of cane or, more correctly, 'centre cane' (so called because it is made from the centre or pulp of the rattan plant). I would recommend using the natural, superior quality. Some of the cheaper varieties are brittle and ragged and consequently far less pleasant to work with. It is very difficult to make good baskets from poor material.

Cane is usually sold in 250g hanks and comes in all sizes from 1mm to 12mm.

Bleached cane is also available. This is very much softer to work with so is more suitable for certain types of work. It dyes well and is particularly good for obtaining light colours. It also turns sharp corners well without cracking or kinking.

Rotacane is a synthetic imitation of centre cane. It is useful in some therapy classes as it comes in a continuous coil and requires no soaking. The finished work does not compare, however, with good-quality centre cane.

Many different materials can be introduced into the weaving to give variety of colour and texture.

PREPARATION

The beauty of centre cane is that it needs little or no preparation. You can just pick it up, dip it in water and begin work when you get the urge.

Cane should not be worked dry or it may crack and you will not be able to shape your basket properly. The smaller sizes usually need only a short dipping in warm water. **Never** leave cane soaking longer than necessary as it will discolour and become rough and ragged.

Always dry thoroughly any unused cane before putting it away and never store your unfinished dampened basket in a plastic bag, or even carry it home from a class in one. If you forget to remove it when you get home the next time you look at it, you may find the cane has developed ugly spots of black mould.

The soaking time needed for the different thicknesses of cane varies from sample to sample. You will soon discover how long is required for the cane to become soft by trying the different grades in warm water.

The preparation of other materials used is explained in the relevant chapter.

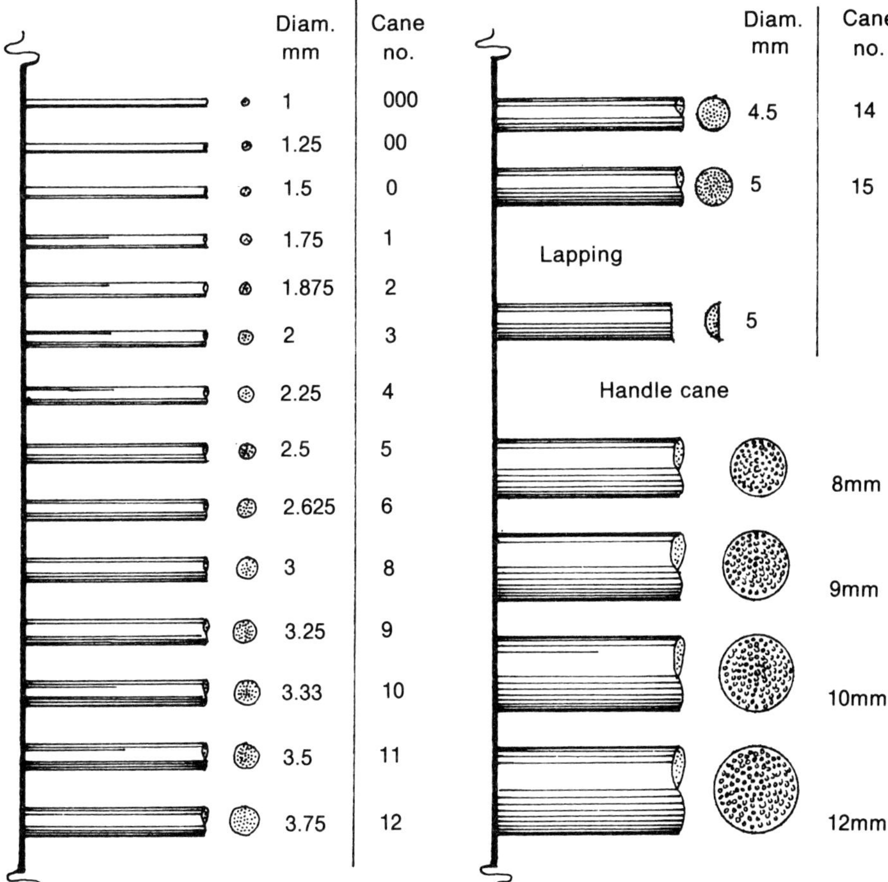

Fig. 1.

FINISHING BASKETS

SINGEING

This can be done to remove the 'hairs'. First damp the basket so that it will not be scorched and, using a butane gas blowtorch, pass the basket to and fro across the flame until all the hairs are singed off.

VARNISH

Sometimes a coat of matt polyurethane varnish will help to firm up a basket and also bring out the different colours.

Coloured polyurethane, such as oak or dark oak, gives cane the appearance of fine willow.

TOOLS

Knife for pointing the ends of the cane and for general use.

Round-nosed pliers used for squeezing the damp cane before bending to prevent splitting when an acute angle is required.

Side cutters for general use throughout the making of a basket and for cutting off the surplus ends.

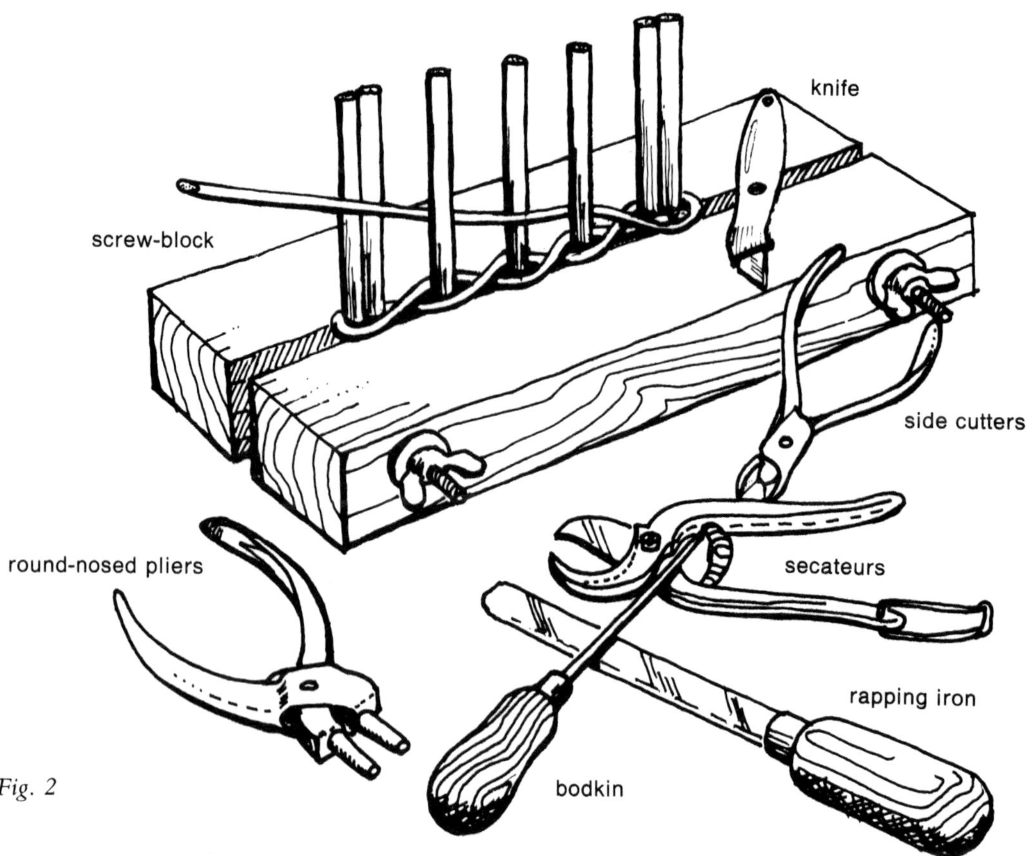

Fig. 2

Bodkin used for splitting base sticks and enlarging spaces in the weaving to insert handles, etc. A knitting needle makes quite a good substitute.

Secateurs for cutting the larger sizes of cane.

Rapping iron can be used (with caution) to tap down the weaving on the side of the basket to keep it even.

A weight approximately 1–2kg (2–4lb) placed inside the basket to steady it while the work is in progress. This can be a scale weight, large stone, etc.

Screw-block illustrated but only used for making square or oblong baskets.

PROJECT 1

Rag basket

This basket is made with a wooden base, a few strips of coloured material, and a relatively small amount of centre cane.

It is simple and fun to make. Angela, my 12-year-old niece, made it beautifully and she had never made a basket before.

If you wish to make the basket with a woven base instead of a wooden one use the instructions for the base of the Fruit Basket. In this case there will be 26 side stakes instead of 27. Work a four-rod wale followed by three rounds of a three-rod wale and then continue with the instructions for the Rag Basket from 'Bye-staking' (p.20).

MATERIALS

For a basket with a 17.75cm (7in) diameter, side height of 10cm (4in) and handle height of 20cm (8in):

- Wooden base with a diameter of 17.75cm (7in) and an uneven number of holes – probably 27
- No. 6 cane for stakes, the upsett, bye-stakes and waling
- No. 8 cane for wrapping the handle
- No. 14 or 15 cane for handle bow and handle liners
- Strips of material (leftovers from dressmaking, etc.) approximately 5cm (2in) wide and 60cm (24in) or more in length

Weight of basket 300g (10oz), approximately 100g (4oz) cane

TOOLS

- Side cutters or secateurs
- Ruler or tape measure
- Bodkin or knitting needle
- Scissors
- Round-nosed pliers
- Bowl for water
- Impact adhesive
- One pin

METHOD

1 Draw several pieces of cane from the bundle of no. 6.

2 Cut lengths of 43cm (17in), one for each hole in the wooden base. This allows 7.5cm (3in) for the foot trac, 10cm (4in) for the side of the basket and 25cm (10in) for the border.

3 Soak in warm water for about five minutes until pliable.

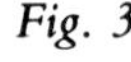
Fig. 3

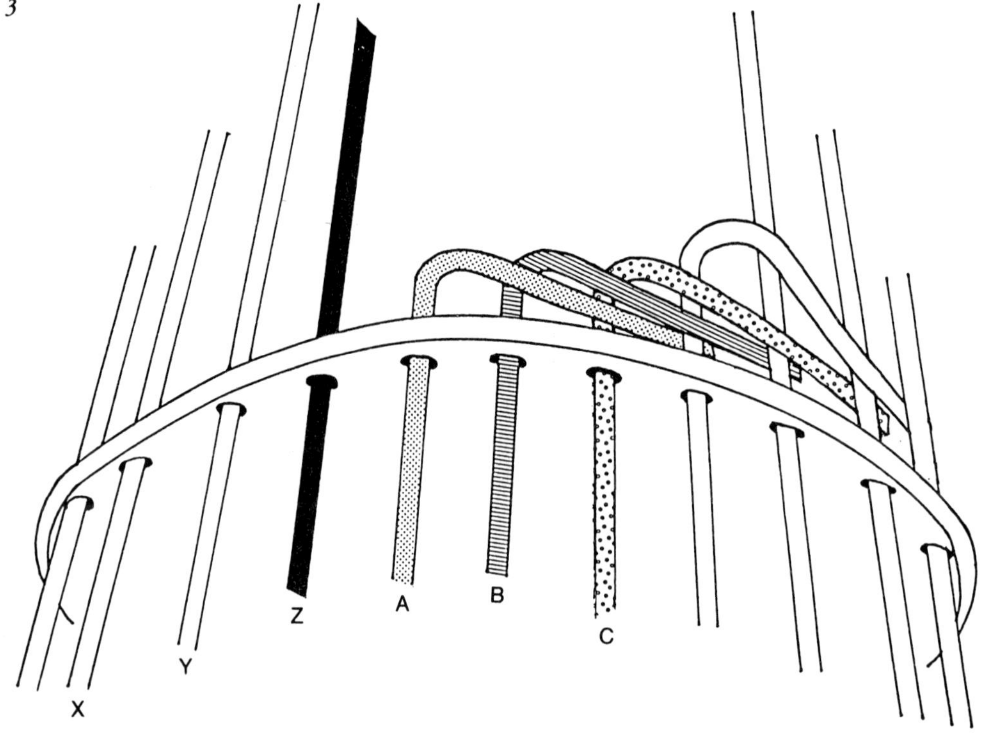

Fig. 4

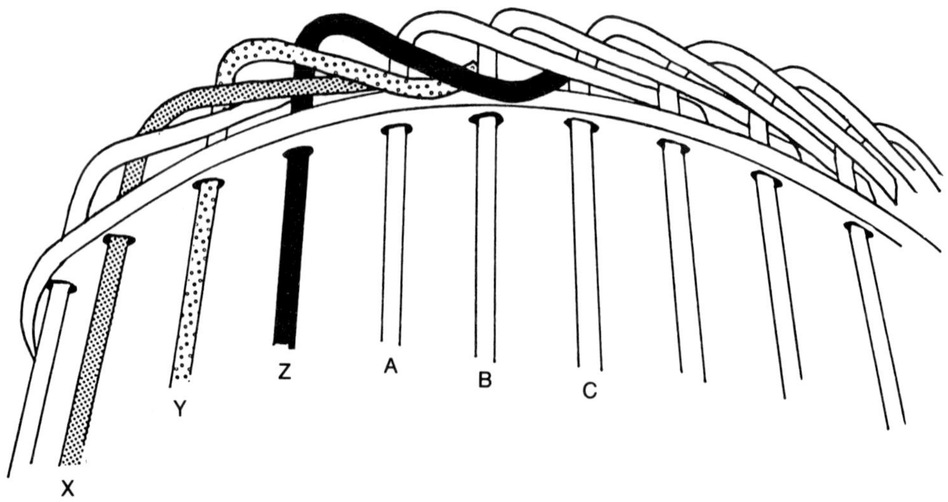

Note The side stakes must be straight. If the cane has been stored wrapped in tight bundles it may need extra soaking in warm water to straighten it out. If this does not work, tie the wet stakes to a broom handle. When dry they will be straight.

FOOT TRAC

1 Hold the base on its edge with the inside facing you. Push the damp stakes through the holes so that approximately 7.5cm (3in) are protruding on the furthest side.

Note If the cane is a very tight fit after it has been soaked, enlarge the holes slightly by inserting a bodkin and giving it a few twists.

2 Bend one of the short ends sideways to the right, take it in front of the next two stakes and tuck it behind the third (fig. 3).

3 Continue round the base, until only three stakes are left unwoven, X, Y and Z.

4 Ease the first three stakes up a little so there is room for Y and Z to be tucked under the start (A & B). Take X first, in front of Y and Z and tuck the end behind A (the first stake you turned down).

5 Next take Y in front of Z and A, and tuck behind B.

6 Finally take Z in front of A and B, tucking it under B so it rests behind C (fig. 4).

Pitfall Make sure that all the ends lying inside on the wooden base project at least 1cm ($\frac{3}{8}$in) behind the next stake, otherwise they may come undone later. If any are too short, ease the stakes through now to make them long enough (fig. 5).

Fig. 5

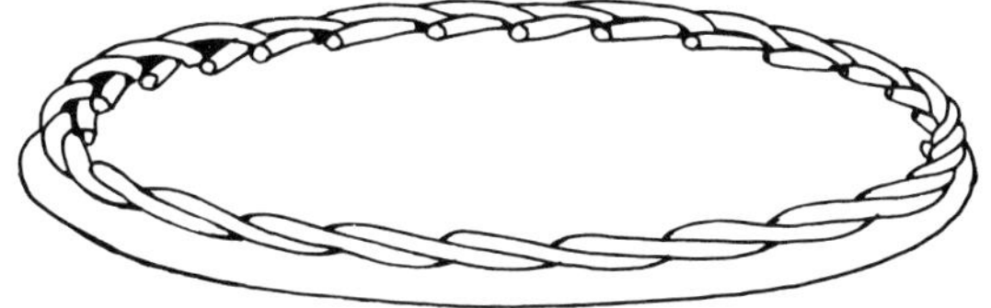

7 This completes the foot trac. Pull all the stakes tight on the upper side, while pushing them from below with your thumb. Bend them outwards slightly so that they begin to create the correct outward flow for the basket.

THE UPSETT (Three-rod wale)

'Three-rod waling' is weaving with three lengths of cane, worked in sequence. It is used to shape and control the stakes, locking them in position with each stroke. 'Waling' is the name of the stroke, but when it is used at the bottom of a basket it is known as the 'upsett'. In this basket three rows of a three-rod wale will be woven to 'set the stakes up' (upsett) in the correct position.

1 Damp three lengths of no. 6 cane, long enough to go three times round the basket with a bit to spare.

Note Damp the cane by dipping it in water. Do not soak it for a long time, as this will spoil the colour and texture.

2 Redamp the stakes if dry and push them gently outwards. The shape of your basket must be planned right from the start.

3 Place a weight inside the base to allow you to use both hands for weaving. A scale weight of about 1–2kg (2–4lb) is about right. Put it in a plastic bag so that it doesn't mark the base.

4 Place a light plastic clothes peg on one of the stakes to act as a marker.

5 Put the three lengths of damp no. 6 cane in three consecutive spaces between stakes – A to the right of the marked stake, B to the right of that, and then C furthest right (the short ends pointing to the left) (see fig. 6).

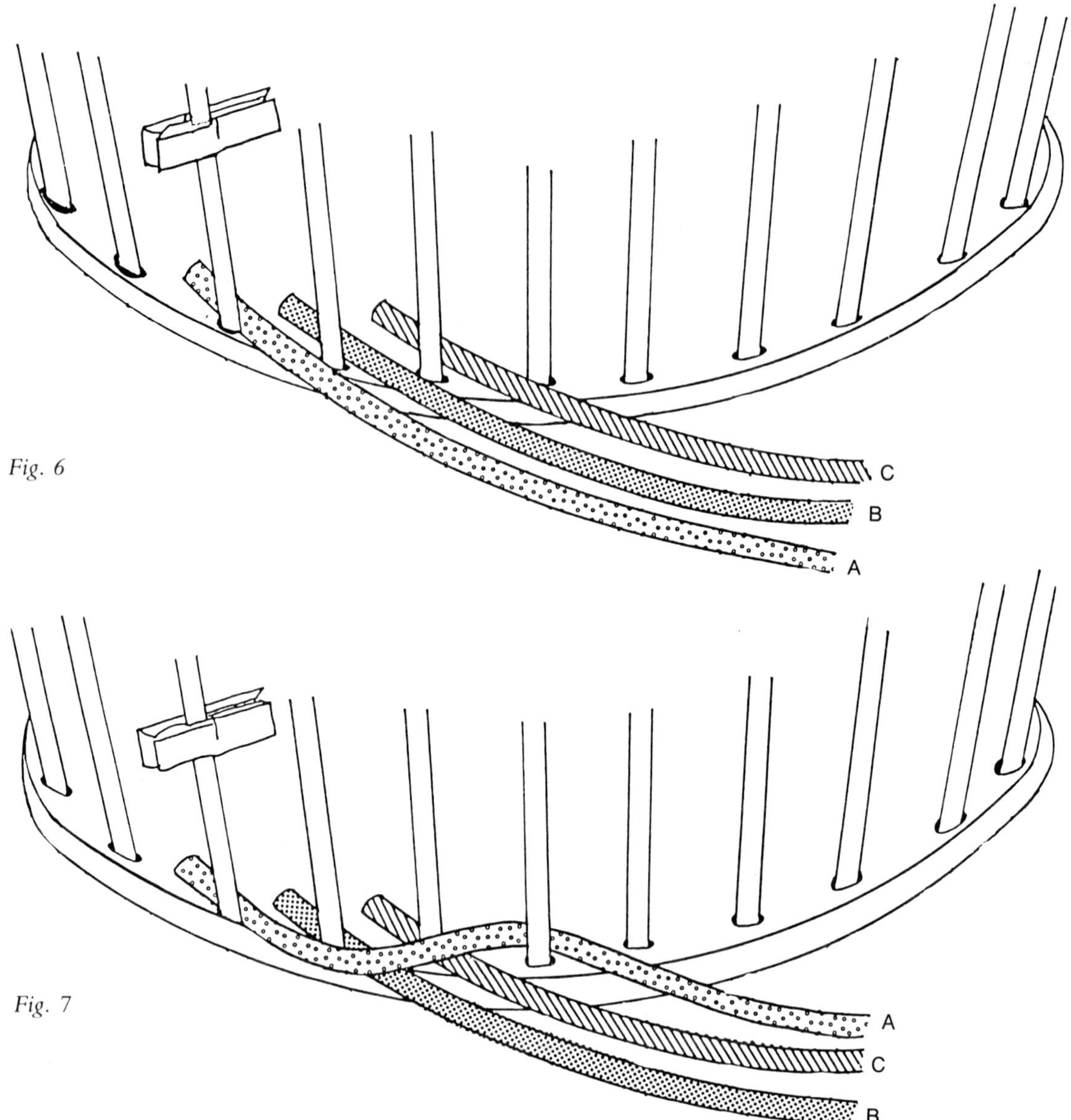

Fig. 6

Fig. 7

The short ends should be just about long enough to lie behind the stake they lean against.

6 Take A in front of two stakes to the right, behind the third and out to the front, being careful not to pull the short end from behind the marked stake (fig. 7).

7 Take B and weave it in front of two stakes, behind one and out to the front (fig. 8).

8 Take C in front of two stakes, behind one and out to the front. Do not pull the cane, handle it lightly. The left hand controls the shape of the basket while the right hand guides the cane in and out of the stakes (fig. 9).

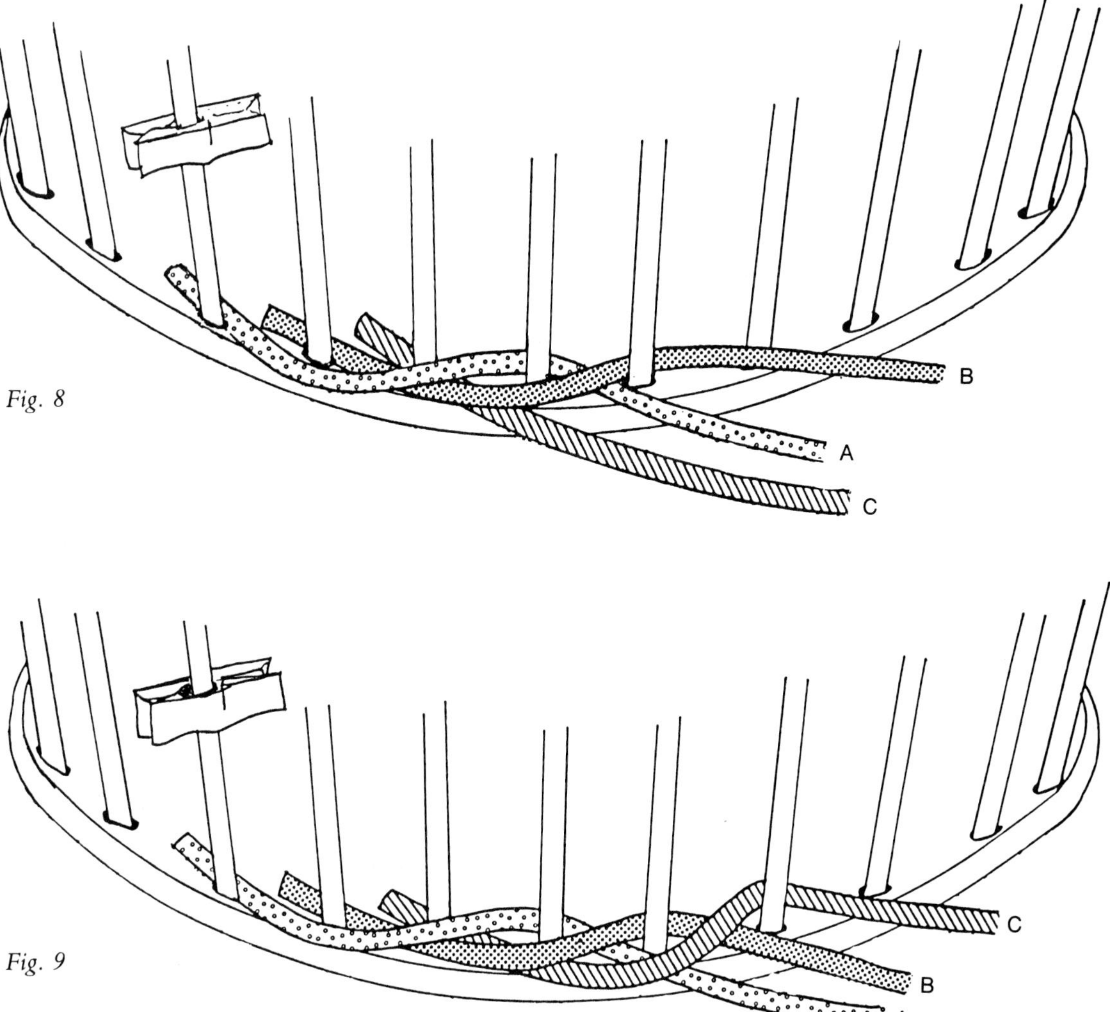

Fig. 8

Fig. 9

9 Weave these three canes in turn, working to the right round the basket. Each stroke is woven 'in front of two and behind one'. I find it easiest to move my left hand so that my index finger is always behind the two stakes when the weaving cane is passed in front of them and brought behind the next stake. This helps to stop the tendency for the stakes to be bent inwards.

The left hand should be continually shaping the basket, adjusting the stakes, seeing they remain upright, not bending to the left or to the right, helping them to flow outwards or to go straight upwards, as required. The left hand should press the weaving firmly down on the last row. Do not forget, it is you who controls the cane, and you can make it do exactly what you want – with practice.

Note Do not worry if you are **left-handed**. Work in exactly the same way as described. The left hand is doing most of the work anyway.

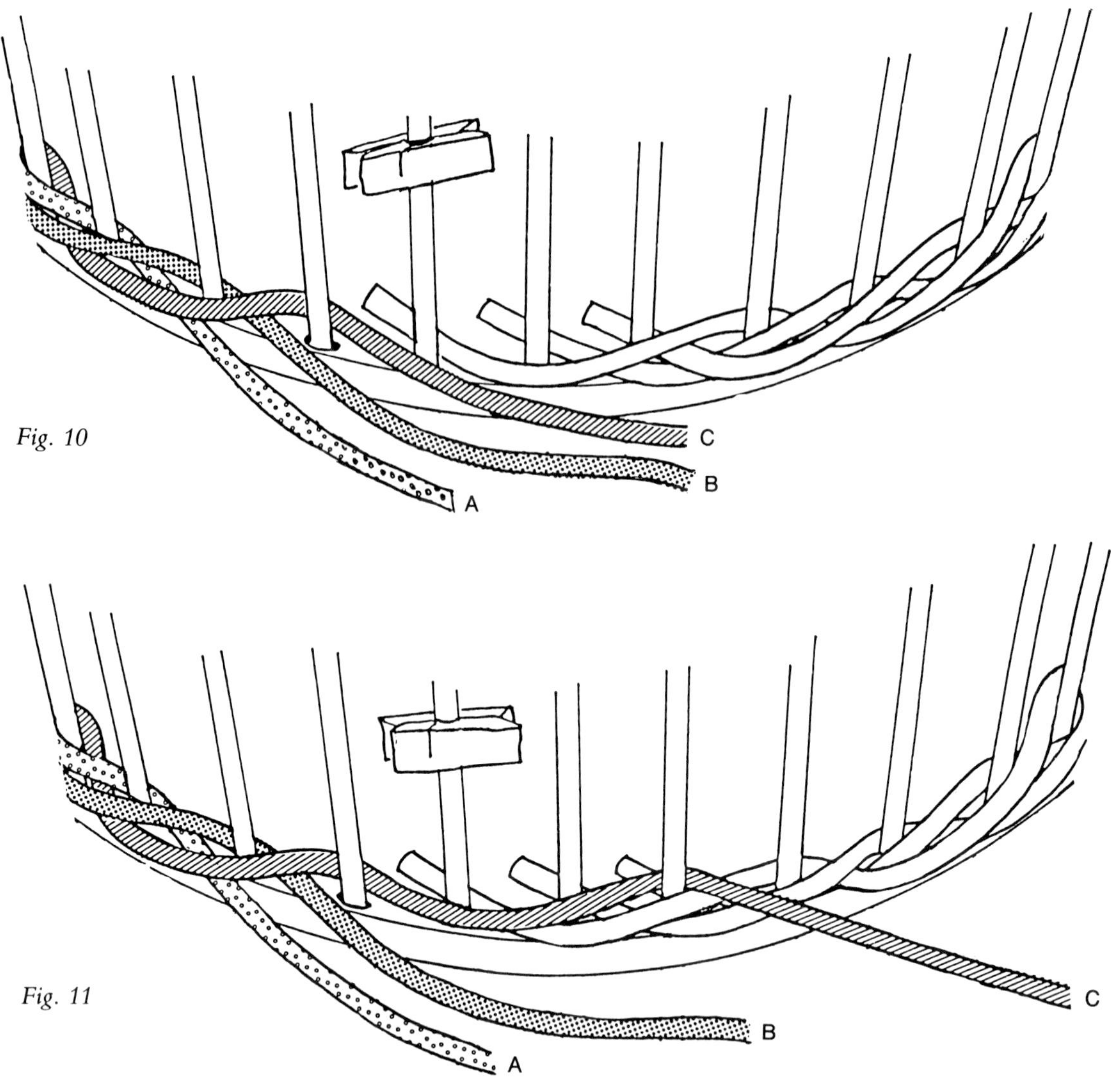

Fig. 10

Fig. 11

CHANGING THE STROKE (or the 'Step-up')

It is necessary to 'change the stroke' to complete each row of waling, otherwise the rows will spiral up on each other leaving a ridge and making it impossible to finish off evenly. (The change-of-stroke is sometimes known as the 'step-up'.)

When the first cane reaches the left-hand side of the marked stake, you have three more strokes to finish the first round of waling. Here, in order to complete the round with no visible difference in the stroke, it is necessary to change the stroke, reversing the order for one stroke each (C, B, A (fig. 10) instead of A, B, C).

1 First take C in front of two, then behind one and out to the front (fig. 11).

2 Take B in front of two, behind one and out to the front (fig. 12).

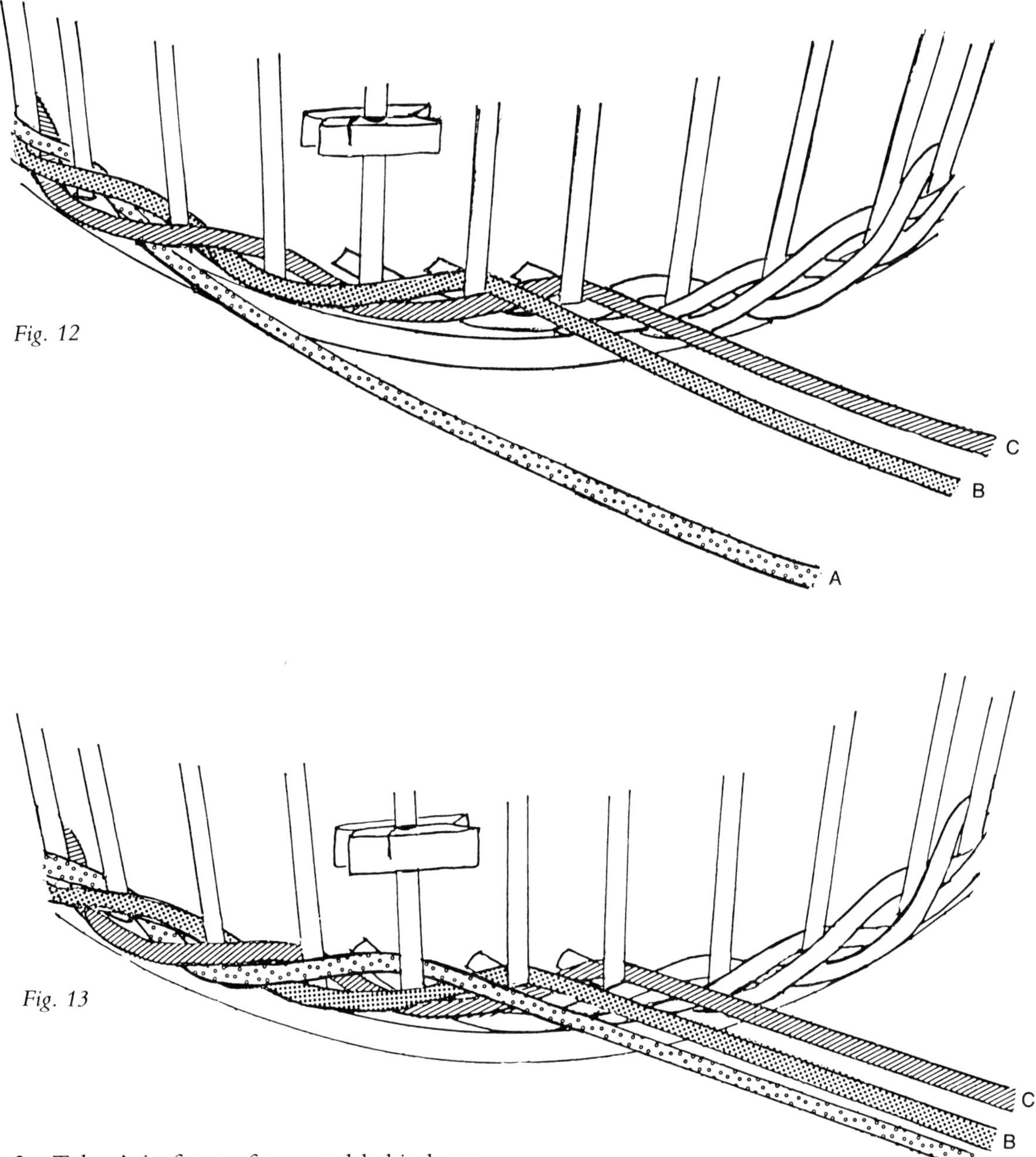

Fig. 12

Fig. 13

3 Take A in front of two and behind one and out to the front. Now you will see that:

- C is lying on top of the starting point of C
- B is lying on top of the starting point of B
- A is lying on top of the starting point of A and is on the right-hand side of the marker (fig. 13).

Your first row of waling is now complete.

Do not worry if the 'stroke' looks different, just check that A, B and C are on top of the three starting ends.

4 Continue with the next round, taking

first A, then B and then C, just as you did at the beginning, but on this row start to bend the stakes outwards slightly so they will be 'upsett' with a slight outward flow. Do not pull the canes you are weaving with, just lay them round the front of two and behind one without distorting the position of the stakes.

5 Continue until you reach the left of the marked stake. Change the stroke exactly as before. When the three moves C, B, A have been completed check that A, B and C lie on the top of the three starting ends on the inside of the basket.

Pitfall Never join in a new cane near the change-of-stroke. It is better to join it in a little early, before the end runs out.

To join waling

The weaver you want to join must be in the left-hand position (A). Pull the old end slightly to the left ('open the door') and slip the new end in beside it and continue weaving. Trim the ends later – one will be outside and one inside (fig. 14).

FINISHING WALING

1 When you have completed the required number of rows (in this case three) and reached the marked stake for the last time, first take A in front of two and behind one and leave the end outside (fig. 15).

2 Next take B in front of two, behind one and **under** one (the previous row) to the front (fig. 16).

3 Finally take C in front of two, behind one and this time under **two** (the previous two rows), bringing the end out to the front (fig. 17).

4 A, B and C now lie under two canes each and in between the same stakes as they did at the start (check this by looking inside for the starting ends). Give each end a little 'tweak' to the left to settle it in the correct position and press the upsett down firmly with your fingers so there are no gaps.

Fig. 14

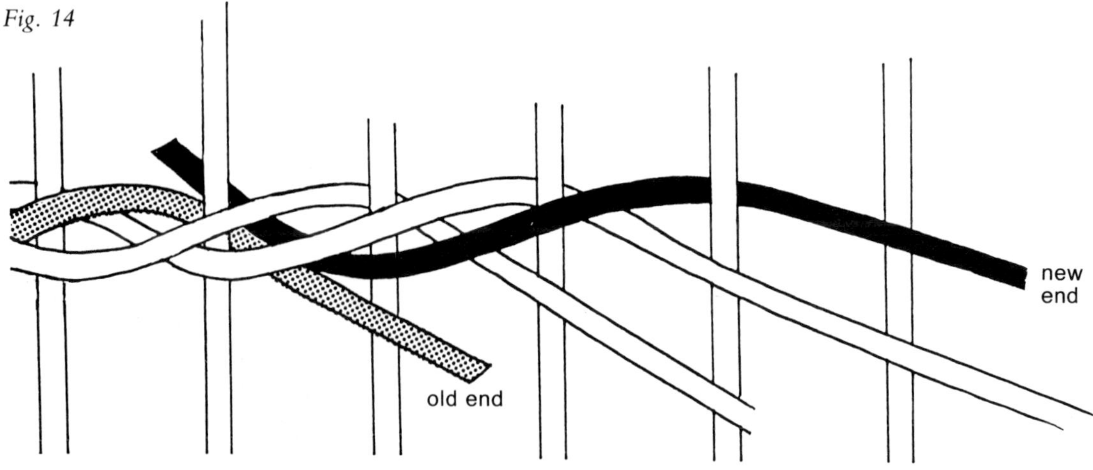

Fig. 15

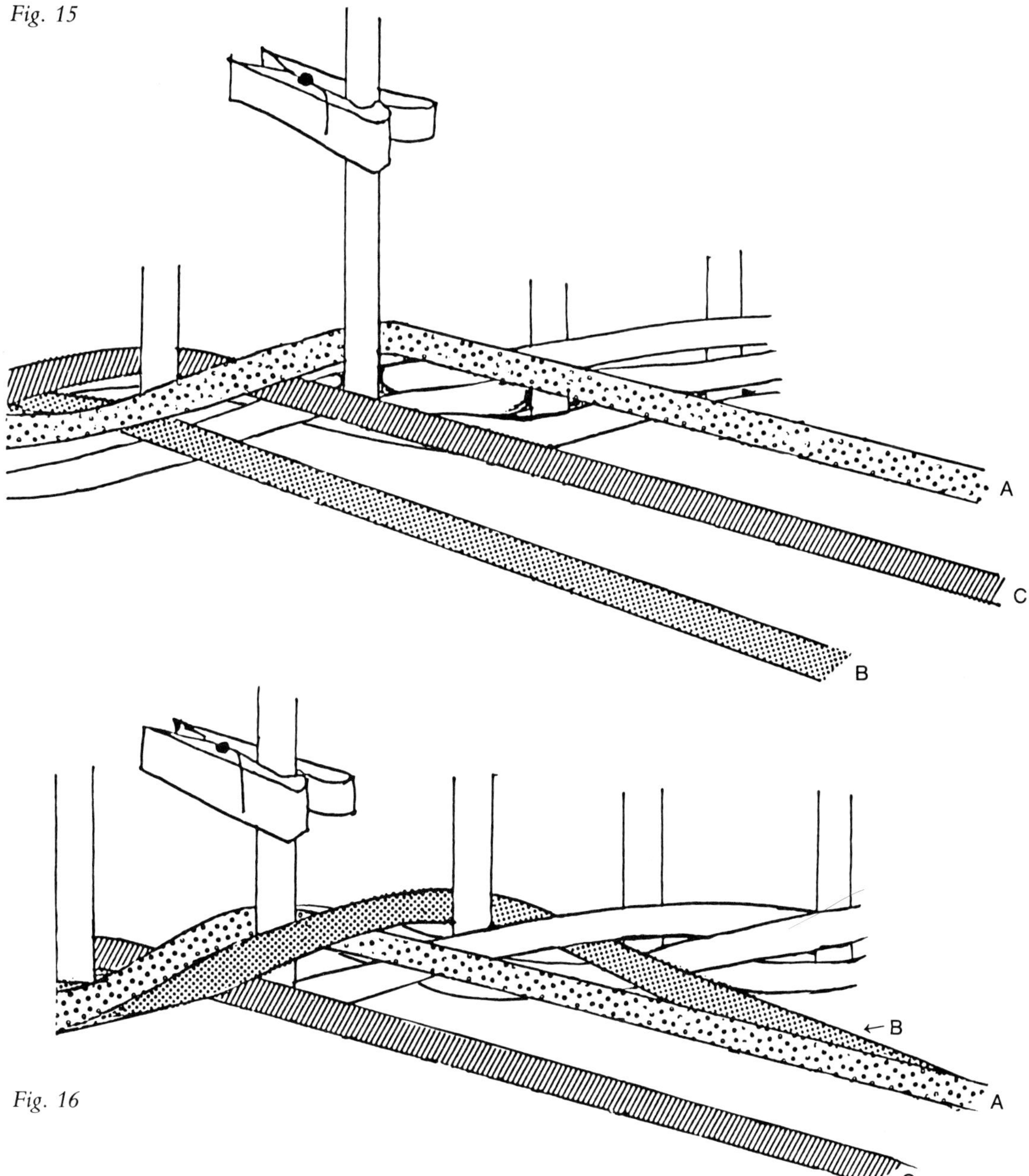

Fig. 16

Trimming the ends

To cut off the ends neatly on the outside, hold the side cutters or secateurs against the side of the basket. Make a slanting cut so that no ends can be felt when you run your hand over the weaving. Trim the inside in a similar way, but make sure the ends are lying against a stake and are **not** cut so short that they pop out to the outside of the basket.

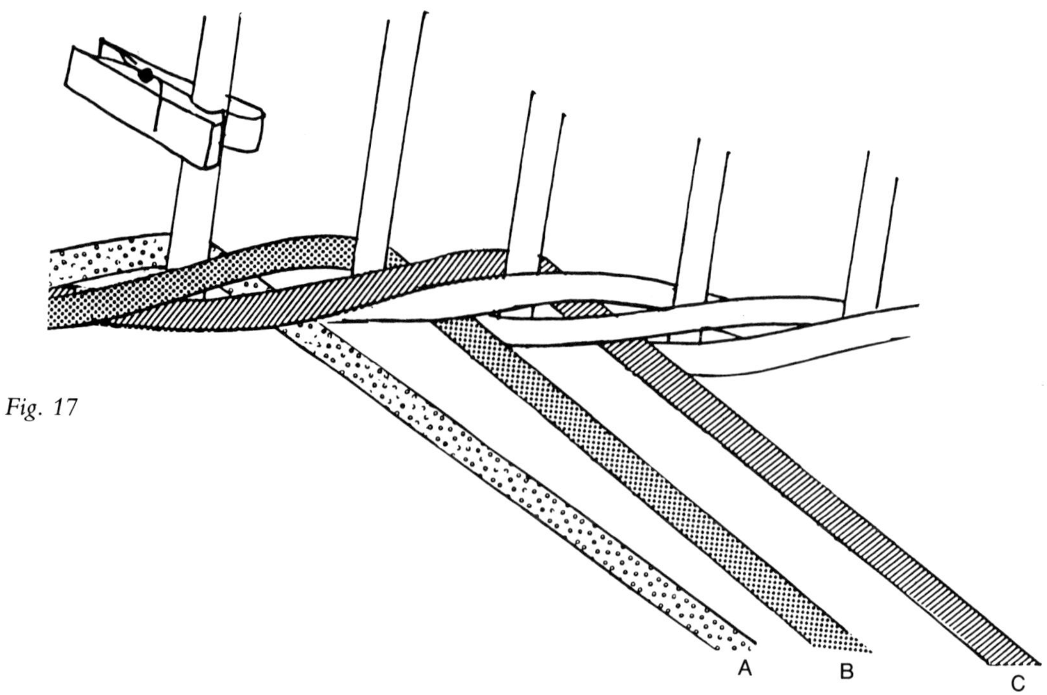

Fig. 17

BYE-STAKING

'Bye-stakes' are second stakes used to strengthen the main stakes and make a firm framework for the basket.

1 From no. 6 cane cut the same number of bye-stakes as there are stakes. Cut each one the height required for the basket, in this case 10cm (4in).

2 Point one end of each bye-stake with a knife or side cutters. Carefully insert a bodkin or knitting needle down into the waling on the right-hand side of each stake, so that the weaving parts a little to allow room for the bye-stake. Now insert the bye-stake which should reach down to the wooden base.

ADDING THE HANDLE LINERS

It is important to add markers for the handle now, as later it will be difficult to insert the handle bow through the material if a channel hasn't already been formed.

Cut two pieces of no. 14 or 15 cane 18cm (7in) long. Point one end of each and push one down between the stake and bye-stake, exactly opposite, on either side of the basket.

PAIRING (using strips of fabric)

'Pairing' is weaving with two lengths of cane, willow or other materials. Each is worked alternately, forming a twist round every stake.

1 Tear lengths of coloured fabric, approximately 5cm (2in) wide, keeping enough over to cover the base if required (see end of instructions, p. 24).

2 Fold over one strip about one-third of the way down its length and loop the fold round a stake and its bye-stake. You now have two lengths to work with, one twice as long as the other (fig. 18).

Fig. 18

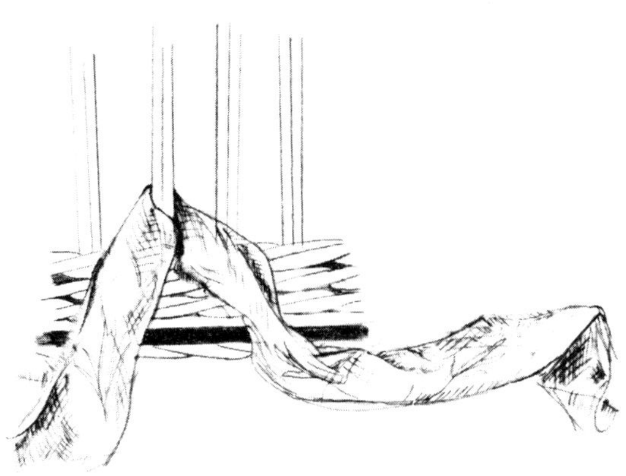

Fig. 19

Note If the material had been folded in half instead of one-third of the way down, both ends would need joining at the same place, which would look a bit bulky. Do not worry about frayed edges, they disappear into the weaving. Any threads can be cut off at the end if necessary.

3 Take the left-hand strip in front of one stake and bye-stake and behind the next, so it crosses over the right-hand strip and now lies to the front again (fig. 19).

4 Take the second strip (which now lies on the left of the pair) and weave it in the same way, 'in front of one and behind one'. Continue weaving round the basket, pushing the material firmly down row upon row.

Joining

Join when the right-hand strip has about 10cm (4in) left. Open it out and place the next strip inside it, overlap about 10cm (4in) and secure **temporarily** with a pin. Weave three more strokes, keeping an eye on the pin.

Remove the pin and continue to pair round the basket, joining in new pieces as necessary and always remember to **remove the pin** before you lose sight of it. (It is better to have only one pin available. Keep the rest out of reach.)

Eleven rows of cotton material will make a block about 6cm ($2\frac{1}{2}$in) deep.

Note Do not make it much deeper than this or the stakes and bye-stakes may be too short for the border. There should be 2cm (¾in) of bye-stake left at this stage.

THREE-ROD WALE

This is the same weave as the upsetting at the beginning of the basket. The three-rod wale gives a strong edge to the top.

1 Take three pieces of damp no. 6 cane. Place the clothes peg as a marker on any stake you choose to start. The first cane goes in the space to the right of the peg, the second and third in the next two consecutive spaces as shown in figs. 6–10.

2 Weave three rows of waling, remembering to change the stroke each time you reach the marker. Push down the rows of waling firmly, compressing the block of pairing below evenly (see figs. 11–13).

3 Finish off the waling as in figs. 15–17. Cut off the ends neatly with side cutters or secateurs. Now measure the height of your basket all the way round from the base to the top of the waling. Tap down any high spots. Next cut off the bye-stakes level with the top of the waling.

Pitfall Be very careful not to cut off the long stake by mistake. To avoid doing just this, pull the stake slightly to the left so that you have room to cut the bye-stake without nicking the stake itself. Press down on the top of the waling with the side cutters, so that the bye-stake is cut as short as possible.

SIMPLE ROLLED BORDER

This is an easy border to manage and can be worked in either two or three simple stages. There are other variations which need slightly longer stakes (see page 24) but for a beginner's basket it might be best to use the least complicated.

1 This is the only tricky part. The stakes for the border have to be soaked so they don't crack when bent over at right angles to form the first part of the border, but you must try not to soak the fabric as it would take a long time to dry out and might turn the cane mouldy. Pour some really hot water into a basin, hold the basket on its side and turn the stakes in the water, carefully watching that you are not soaking further than the top wale.

2 To test when the stakes are pliable enough, bend the top 1cm of one stake at a right angle – if it bends without cracking you can start the border – if not soak for longer.

First Stage

1 Squeeze each stake close to the top of the waling with the round-nosed pliers and then bend each one over carefully to the right. Do not hurry this as you want each stake to bend without cracking.

2 Working round the border, take each stake down behind the next one to the right, and out to the front (fig. 20).

3 To finish the first stage, tuck the last stake through the loop formed by the first stake.

Second Stage

1 Now take all the states to the inside. Pick up any stake, pass it in front of the two stakes to its right and over two horizontal ends, and then under the second loop to the inside (fig. 21).

2 Continue round the border, working to the right and threading each end to the inside. Thread away the last two in sequence.

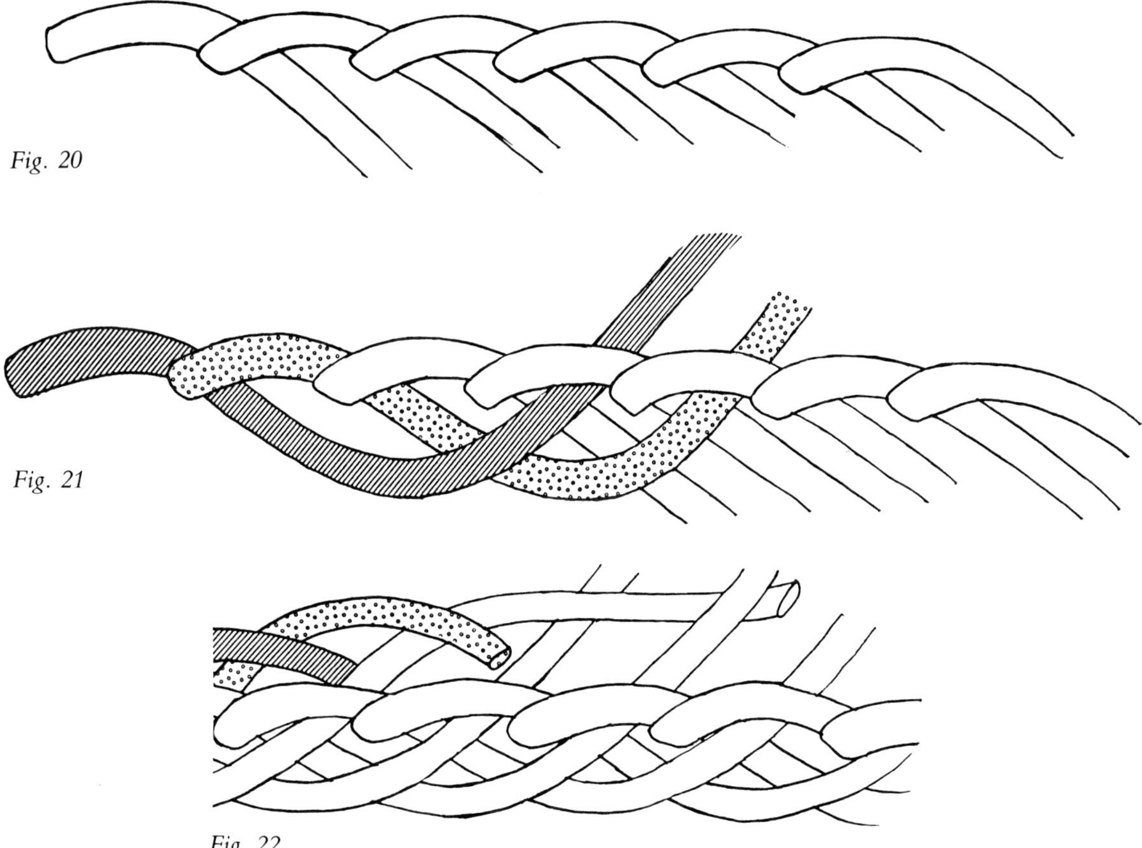
Fig. 20

Fig. 21

Fig. 22

Third Stage (optional – see second note)

1 Hold the basket in your lap to finish off the border on the inside. Working from left to right take each stake in turn over the end of the one to its right, and leave it tucked in behind the next (fig. 22).

2 Continue round the inside until the last stake. This is tucked in under the first loop.

Note Steps 1 and 2 of the third stage can be repeated if the ends are long enough and you have enough patience; this makes a neat, strong rolled finish. Another alternative with long enough ends is to take each one in front of two instead of in front of one before tucking it behind the next.

3 All the ends can now be cut off neatly inside, but be sure you do not cut them too short or they may come undone later on. Each one should be firmly tucked against the inside of the basket with about 1cm protruding below the finished border.

Note If the third stage presents difficulties and as long as the stakes are not more than 2–3cm ($\frac{3}{4}$–$1\frac{1}{2}$in apart), the ends can be cut off on the inside after the first two stages have been completed, but be sure the ends lie against a stake on the inside and have at least a 1.5cm ($\frac{3}{4}$in) tail left for security.

THE HANDLE

1 Cut a piece of no. 14 or 15 cane 50cm (20in) long and point both ends. Pull out one of the handle liners and gently replace it with one end of the handle cane, easing it down to the base without distorting the material. Now do the same with the other end and check that the handle is the right height – mine measures about 20cm (8in) up from the bottom of the basket.

2 Make a plait from three pieces of the same material as used for the basket. Tie one end with some string to a table leg (or other immovable object) to make working easier.

Ensure that the plait is long enough to cover the handle and that there are at least 15cm (6in) of unplaited material at each end to make the final bows or knots.

3 Spread a little impact glue along the top edge of the handle and on the underside of the plait. Position the two together, remembering to leave enough material at each end of the plait, and secure firmly.

4 Damp a length of no. 8 cane so that it is really pliable. Point one end and push it down into the waling beside one end of the handle bow. Wrap it four times round the bow and the plait, finishing on the inside of the basket at the other end of the handle. Now take it under the waling to the outside and back over the handle the opposite way, so it forms crosses with the first strand (see colour photograph).

Finish with the end on the inside and weave it in and out under the waling for a few strokes before cutting it off.

PEGGING THE HANDLE

Handle bows must always be pegged or tacked to stop them coming loose.

1 Drive a bodkin obliquely through the waling and the handle from outside to inside.

Cut a 5cm (2in) piece of no. 6 cane to a point. Put a touch of glue on it and, removing the bodkin, tap the cane peg through so it is visible on the inside of the basket. Do the same on the other side of the handle (see fig. 49).

2 Cut off the ends neatly. The handle is now secure.

3 Knot the ends of the fabric or tie in a bow if long enough.

OPTIONAL EXTRA

If you have made this basket with the wooden base and would like to cover it with some material, cut a cardboard circle the size of the inside of the basket and find a piece of material large enough to cover the card leaving a 5cm (2in) overlap all round. Run a gathering thread in and out of the material 2cm (1in) from the edge. Lay the cardboard on the material and pull the thread tight so the card is neatly covered. Fasten the thread off securely. Put the circle into the base of the basket and stand back and admire your work!

ROLLED BORDER VARIATIONS

(by kind permission of Flo Hoppe, see Bibliography)

A **1** Behind two and out to the front.
2 In front of three and in.
3 Over two and down.

(The length of the stakes above the waling needs to be ten times the distance between any two stakes.)

B **1** Behind two and out.
2 In front of three and in.
3 Over two and down.

(Add another row to make an attractive roll inside.)

4 Over two and down.

(The length required is 14 times the distance between stakes.)

C **1** In front of **two** and in.
2 Over two and down.
3 Over two and down.

(The length required is 12 times the distance between stakes.)

D **1** In front of **three** and in.
2 Over two and down.
3 Over two and down.

(The length required is 14 times the distance between stakes.)

PROJECT 2

Fruit basket with scalloped border

This basket is designed to be a follow-on project from the Rag Basket. It has a woven base (but could be made with a wooden base, see end of chapter), a simple scalloped border and a foot trac.

MATERIALS

For a basket 12.5cm (5in) in height, with diameters of 18cm (7in) at the base and 20cm (8in) at the top:

- No. 12 cane for the base sticks
- No. 3 cane for pairing the base and randing the side.
- No. 6 cane for the side stakes, bye-stakes and waling

I used natural and dyed cane for this basket. The sides could be paired with strips of material (as in the Rag Basket), substituting pairing for the randing. If using natural cane throughout, the basket could be stained with wood stain – a mixture of Dark Oak and Mahogany gives a colour which looks similar to buff willow. Matt polyurethane varnish will seal the stain, without making it look too shiny.

Weight of basket 125g ($4\frac{1}{2}$oz)

METHOD

MAKING A WOVEN BASE

The base could be paired in two different colours (see end of chapter).

1 Cut six pieces of no. 12 cane 23cm (9in) long. (These will be the base sticks.)

2 Mark the middle of three of the pieces.

3 Working on a wooden board, push the bodkin through the marks so that all three sticks are threaded on the bodkin (fig. 23).

If you find this difficult, make a little slit with a craft knife in the middle of the sticks and thread them one at a time onto the bodkin.

Note Work carefully on a board so you do not make holes in the table or yourself!

4 Now push two of the other canes through the slit, one on either side of the bodkin. Remove the bodkin and push the third stick through in its place. The cross which is formed is called the 'slath' (fig. 24).

5 Soak the slath in warm water for five minutes, or until pliable.

Fig. 23

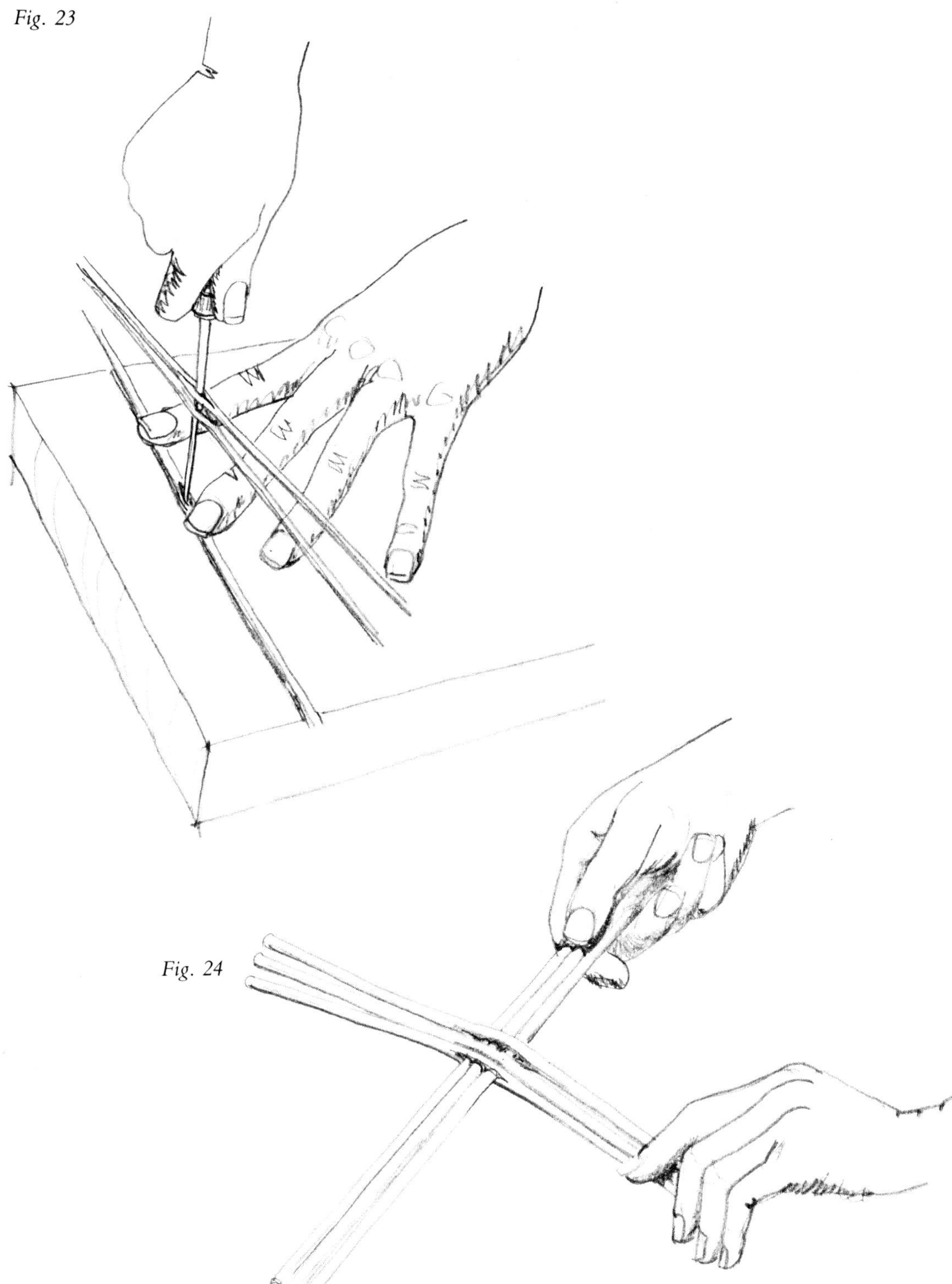

Fig. 24

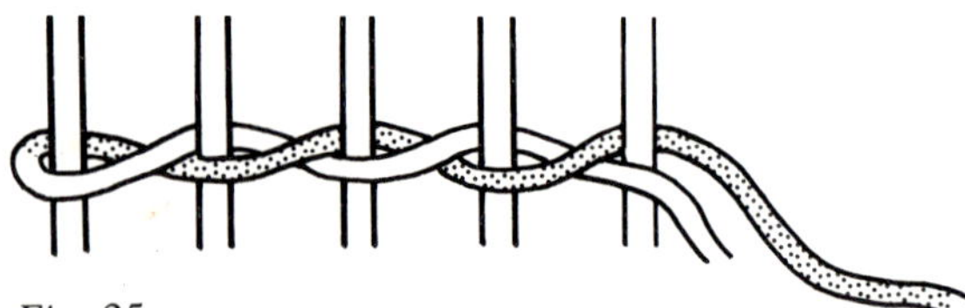

Fig. 25

TYING IN THE SLATH (Pairing)

'Pairing' is weaving with two lengths of cane (or other material), worked alternately to form a twist (fig. 25). Start with one piece of cane bent in two (in the same way you used the strip of material for the Rag Basket).

1 Damp a length of no. 3 cane.

2 Squeeze it with round-nosed pliers at the point you wish it to bend, so that it won't crack. This should be done about one-third of the way along so that as you work both ends will not run out together.

Note Another way of bending a piece of **soaked** cane sharply without breaking it is to hold the cane firmly with the index finger and thumb of both hands at the point where the bend is required. Twist in opposite directions and then bend the cane.

3 Hold the slath in your left hand, with the four groups of bottom sticks pointing north, south, east and west. Loop the no. 3 cane behind 'north' and hold in place with your index finger (fig. 26).

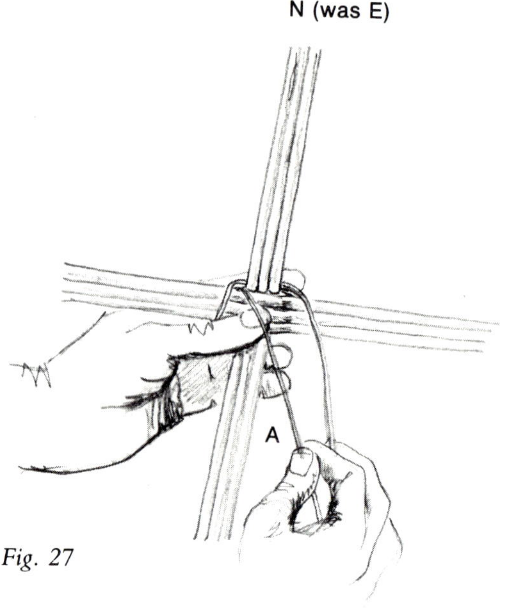

Fig. 27

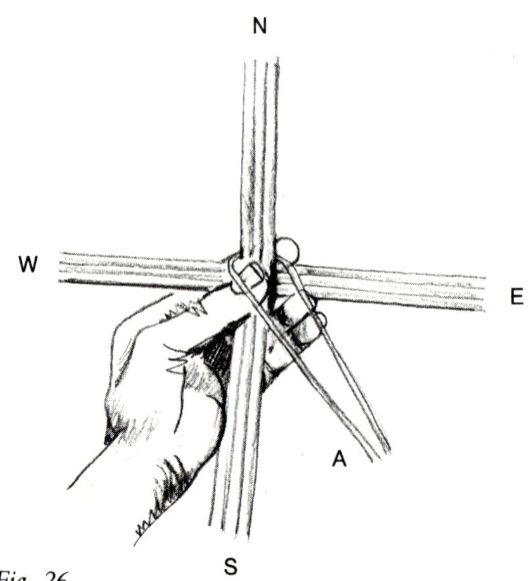

Fig. 26

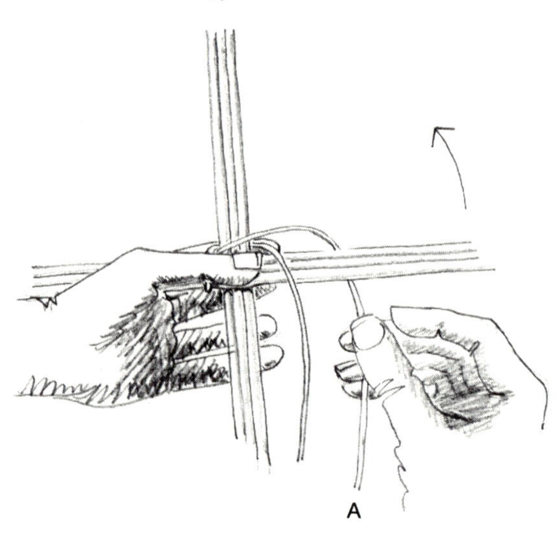

Fig. 28 and now turn

4 Take the left of the pair of canes, A, firmly in front of 'north', behind 'east' and back to the front.

5 Turn the slath a quarter turn anti-clockwise, so that 'east' becomes 'north' and the two canes which you are pairing with are in the same positions as at the beginning (fig. 27).

6 Take A (A is always the cane on the left) in front of 'north', behind 'east' and back to the front. Turn the slath a quarter turn anti-clockwise (fig. 28).

7 Repeat steps 4–6 and continue pairing round the slath in this way until each group of three sticks has two strands of pairing tying it together.

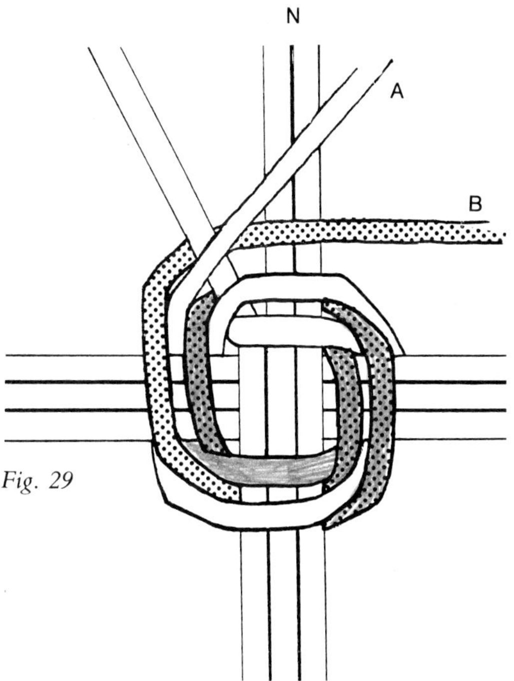

Fig. 29

OPENING OUT THE SLATH

1 Open out the left-hand stick of the group 'north' and bring B (which was lying at the **back**) to the front through the gap created, so that both A and B are lying towards you (fig. 29).

2 Now take A firmly to the back through the same gap.

3 Pull A down tightly on to B.

4 Open out the right-hand stick of the group. Bring A to the front again through the gap (it now becomes B as it is the right-hand one of the pair).

5 Continue pairing round the slath, opening out the sticks into singles as you go. As you work, try to get the sticks evenly spaced and all on the same plane (not corrugated).

Note In order to get the base really tightly woven, there are two distinct movements when pairing, especially at the beginning of a base. The first is to take A **firmly** to the back, pulling it down tightly onto B – pause – and then **gently** to the front again (these two movements will help to 'crown' the base – see below). It may help to push the cane down between the sticks with the tip of a bodkin during the first row of opening out, in order to get it really tight.

Joining pairing

After five or six rows it will be necessary to join. To do this thread the end of a new cane from the front underneath and to the left of the old end so that it rests against the left-hand base stick, leaving about 2cm ($\frac{3}{4}$in) at the back to be cut off later. Take the new end over the top of the old and carry on pairing (fig. 30).

(Fig. 31 shows an alternative method of joining.)

CROWNING THE BASE

A woven basket base should be slightly curved, like a saucer turned upside down

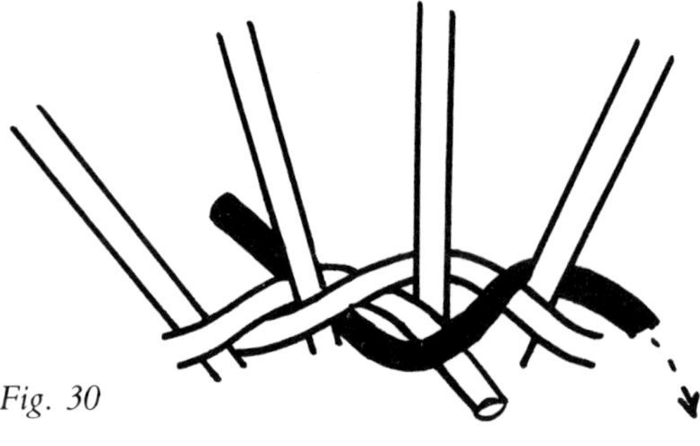
Fig. 30

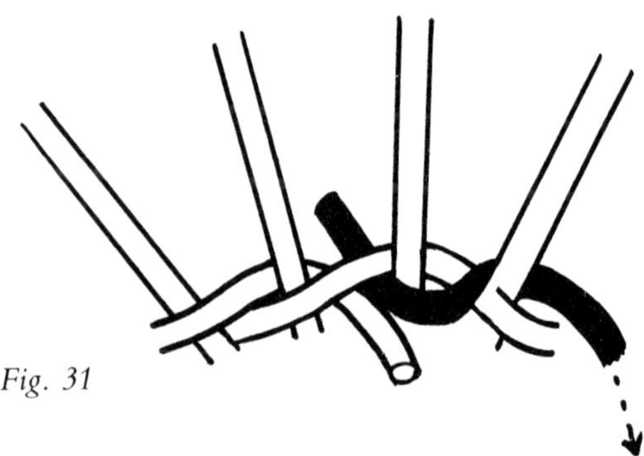
Fig. 31

(but not with as much curve as an umbrella!), so that when the basket is finished it will stand firmly on the rim of the base.

After about six rounds start to crown the base. As you pair round, gently but firmly shape the base sticks so they curve **away** from you. Continue to make sure the spaces between the sticks are even, adjusting with every stroke.

FINISHING THE BASE

When the base measures 18cm (7in) in diameter finish by tucking the last end under the previous row and out to the front.

STAKING UP

'Staking up' is pushing the side stakes into the base.

1 Cut 48 side stakes of 43cm (17in) from no. 6 cane. (I used 24 dyed turquoise and 24 dark oak – see end of chapter for dyeing instructions.)

2 Point one end of each stake with a knife or side cutters (basketmakers call this a 'slype').

3 Soak about 10cm (4in) of the slyped end in warm water for five to ten minutes. The easiest way to do this is to stand the stakes in a jar of warm water. If you are using dyed cane, wipe with a cloth or tissue to remove any loose dye after soaking.

Trimming the ends

If the base of your basket is firmly and tightly woven you can cut off all the ends of the bottom sticks close to the edge before staking up. If it is slightly loose it might be safer to cut them off one at a time while staking up, as suggested below.

Pitfall Do **not** cut the ends from the pairing joins **until** the stakes are in place.

4 Turn the base concave side uppermost, so it stands like a saucer right way up.

5 Using a bodkin (or knitting needle) to make a channel, insert the slyped end of one stake well down into the base beside one of the bottom sticks. It is very important to drive in the stake as far as possible, otherwise it may come loose when the upsetting is started. Now cut off the protruding end of the bottom stick and insert a stake well down into the pairing on its other side. Repeat around the base (fig. 32).

Note Most baskets have only one side stake on each side of a bottom stick. However, for this pattern with a scalloped border two are needed.

6 Widen the gap on each side and push the second set of slyped stakes in place one on either side of those already inserted. You will find that they will not go down quite so far as the first stakes.

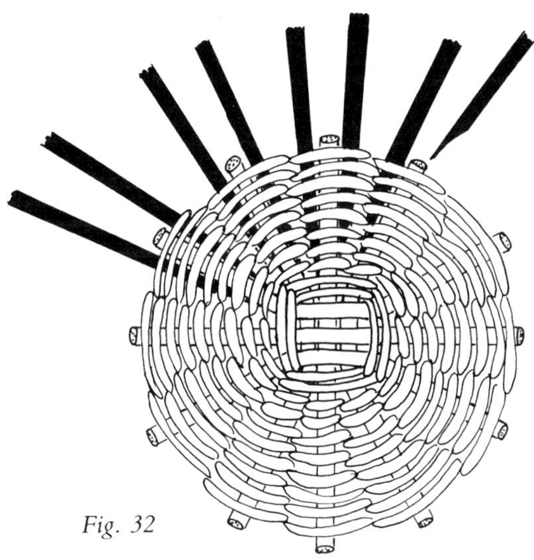
Fig. 32

7 Continue round the base, inserting two more stakes on each side of the bottom sticks.

8 Now trim any ends so that the base is smooth.

PRICKING UP THE STAKES

Prior to starting the upsett you will need to bend the stakes at a right angle to the base. This is known as 'pricking up'. Willow workers do this by pricking the rods with a knife. Cane workers squeeze the stakes with round-nosed pliers.

1 When all the stakes are firmly in place turn the base right side up (upside-down saucer). Squeeze the **damp** stakes with round-nosed pliers at the point where they merge from the base, so they will bend up at a right angle without breaking (fig. 33).

Note Bend the first stake up very carefully. If a crack appears soak the base and the stakes a little longer until they are really pliable.

2 Secure all the ends together with string or an elastic band (the ones the postmen bring are ideal!).

THE UPSETT (Four-rod wale)

The upsett of a basket with a woven base starts with a four-rod wale. This has three purposes: to fill in the gap which would otherwise be visible between the edge of the base and the side of the basket; to separate the pairs of stakes evenly; and to make a rim for the basket to stand on.

One round of the four-rod wale is followed by three rows of a three-rod wale, which control the ultimate shape of the basket.

1 Take two full lengths of no. 6 cane, well soaked in warm water for a minute or two.

2 With the basket on its side on your lap, loop the canes round two pairs of stakes as in figs. 34–35, leaving one pair between the loops. (Single stakes shown for clarity).

3 Mark the stake to the left of the first loop (with a clothes peg, twist-tie or

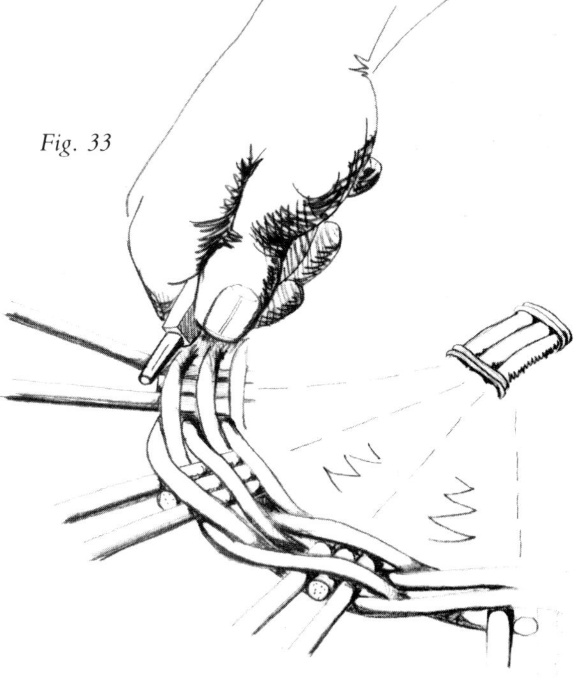
Fig. 33

something eye-catching). Work a four-rod wale – start as for the three-rod wale (see figs. 6–9), but each time take the left-hand cane (A) in front of **three** (pairs) and behind the fourth (instead of in front of **two** and behind the third as in a three rod-wale).

Note This first row of waling, woven with four canes after staking up the base, is a 'pull-down' wale. Holding the basket on its side, separate each group of four stakes by easing the left-hand pair to the left and the right-hand pair to the right as you weave, pulling down firmly between the left stake (of each pair) and the edge of the base, then **round** the end of the base stick and behind the right hand pair of stakes.

The 'pull-down' helps to separate the pairs of stakes and prevent a gap forming between the base and the upsetting. See this four-rod wale as the finishing round for the base rather than the start of the side (fig. 34).

4 When the marked stake is reached, weave A round it and leave this rod to its right (A has now become D as it is the furthest right) (fig. 35).

5 Change the stroke (step up) with the next three weavers, taking C then B and finally A, still working in front of three pairs of stakes and behind one.

6 Cut off D leaving an end of at least 7.5cm (3in). Cut off any loose ends from joins on the base so they do not catch on the working surface and thread the end of D to the inside of the basket.

THE UPSETT (Three-rod wale)

1 Now sit the basket on its base and put a weight inside.

2 Continuing with A, B and C, work a three-rod wale (in front of two pairs and behind one), spacing the pairs evenly as you work, and pressing the rows firmly down with your fingers. Remember to change the stroke each time the mark is reached (see figs. 10–13). After one or two rounds undo the string or elastic band, and if the stakes stand up nicely you can leave them untied while you complete the third row of the three-rod wale.

3 As you work round the basket, pull the stakes out gently so that the correct angle with a slight outward flow is obtained. The rows of waling do tend to bend in at the change-of-stroke, so try to ease them out at this point as you work.

4 On reaching the mark, and having done one row of four-rod and three rows of three-rod, finish waling as in figs. 15–17.

Note If the stakes are still not very well 'set up' even after the four rows of waling, put on another row or two until the stakes

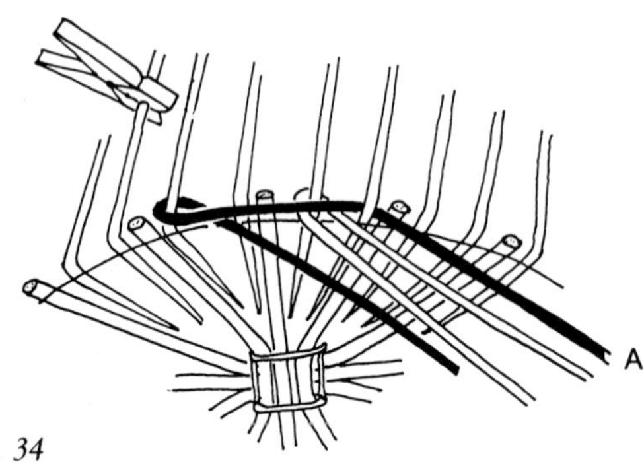

Fig. 34

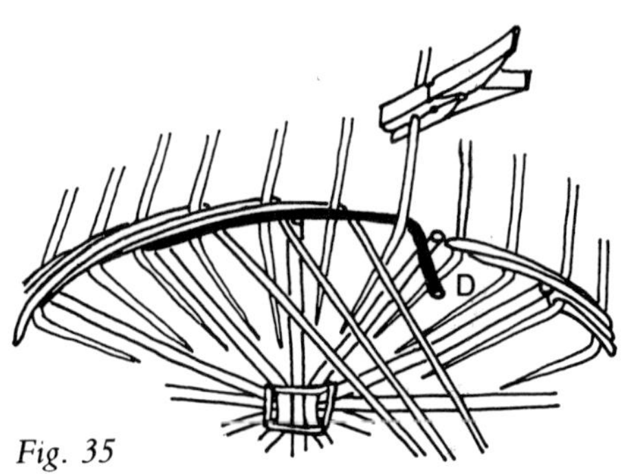

Fig. 35

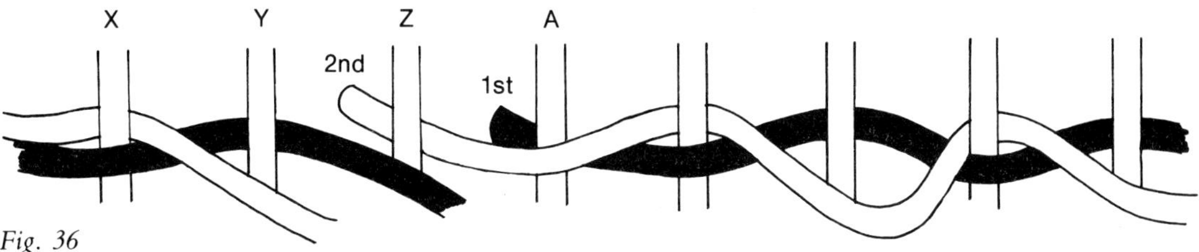

Fig. 36

are standing firmly upright and the foundation of your basket is sound.

5 After finishing off correctly, cut off the ends neatly with the side cutters.

RANDING

This is a simple weave – the length of cane is woven in and out of the stakes, in front of one and behind the next (fig. 38). With an uneven number of stakes it is possible to work round and round the basket in this manner, only taking a new piece of cane when it is necessary to join.

However, because this basket has an **even** number of stakes, it is not possible to rand with a single length, as each time round the basket the weaver would go in front and behind the same stakes. In order to rand correctly, two lengths of cane will be used, one following the other. This is known as 'follow-on randing', or 'chasing weave'.

Follow-on randing

1 Take a length of no. 3 cane and dip it in water. No. 3 cane is used because it is only half the thickness of no. 6, which was used for the stakes. You must always weave the side of your basket with a thinner cane than that used for the stakes, otherwise your basket will be pushed out of shape by the weavers 'ruling' the stakes.

2 Place a weight inside the basket.

3 Tuck the end of the cane inside the basket behind stake A as in fig. 36 (a pair of stakes in this basket).

4 Place the index finger of your left hand on the end of the cane to hold it in place, weave in front of the next pair of stakes to the right, and behind the next.

Note As you work, turning the basket round, put the tip of the index finger of your left hand behind the stakes you are weaving across. Ease the stakes out slightly,

Fig. 37

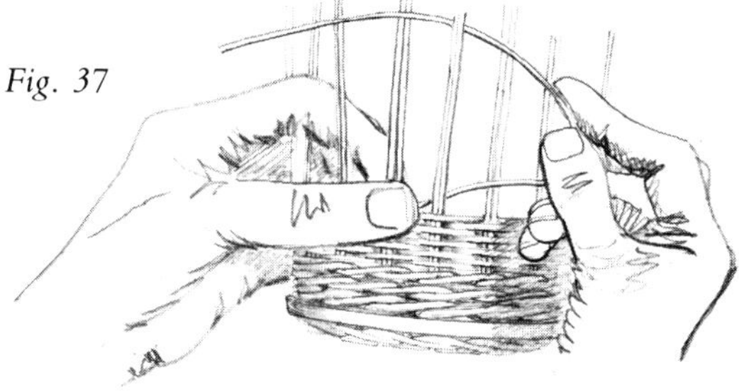

Fig. 38

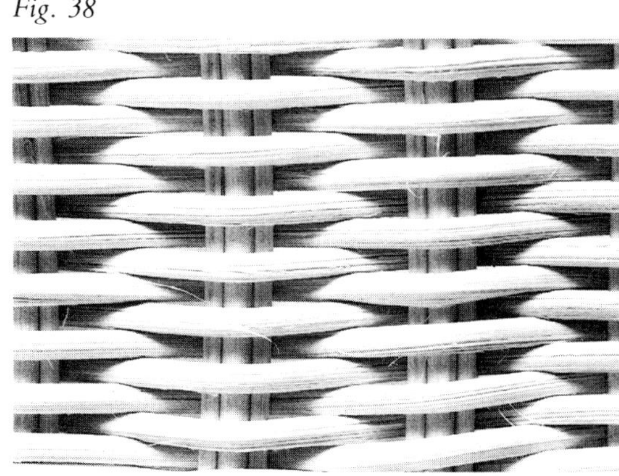

loop the cane through the next gap, hold it with the left thumb, then pull the loop out to the front with the index finger and thumb of the right hand (see fig. 37).

5 Continue to rand round in this way, in front of one pair of stakes and behind the next, leaving the end between Y and Z (see fig. 36).

6 Start a second piece of cane in the next space, between Z and A (see fig. 36) so that it is woven in and out of the opposite stakes from the last row. Rand round until the end of the first length is reached. Do not overtake it. Stop one space to the left (between stakes X and Y – see fig. 36). Pick up the first cane and carry on randing for one round until you reach the stake to the left of the end of the second weaver. Continue to rand in and out, shaping with the left hand, making sure the stakes are parallel to each other and are not being pulled inwards too much.

Pitfall **Never** overtake the previous row. Catch up and then go on with the second weaver. The lower of the two weavers is ahead all the time.

Joining

The join used in randing is simple. Both ends are left behind the same stake. Fig. 39 shows the join on the inside of the basket.

Note Try not to have too many joins near each other. Afterwards they must be trimmed carefully – long enough to rest inside against a stake but short enough for the inside to feel smooth to your hand.

Fig. 39

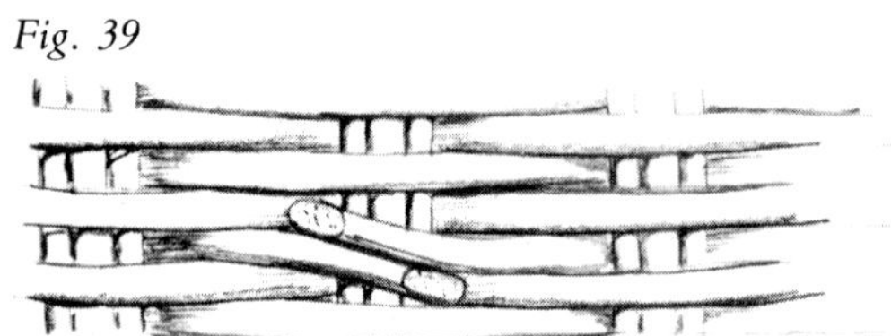

7 Continue with the follow-on randing, handling the cane lightly. Do not pull at this stage as that will cause the sides to start flowing inwards (and will be tiring for your fingers). However, when you have woven about 2cm ($\frac{3}{4}$in), if you **would** like the sides to start curving in slightly (see the colour photo), give a little pull after each stroke, and bend the stakes slightly inwards as you work. The harder you pull the sharper the curve will be.

8 When the randing measures 4cm ($1\frac{1}{2}$in), which is about 18 rows, finish off the two ends next to each other, laying them behind consecutive stakes.

THREE-ROD WALE

Damp three pieces of no. 6 cane and put on two or three rows of waling to give a strong edge to the top of the basket. Follow instructions on pages 14–20.

SCALLOPED BORDER

1 Point the ends of all the stakes with side cutters.

2 Take one pair behind the next pair to the right and across in front of the next (see colour photograph).

3 Carefully run a bodkin or knitting needle down the rows of waling, so it comes out at the base of the basket.

4 Push the pointed ends of the first pair down through the space the bodkin has created, and pull gently so there is a loop of about 4cm ($1\frac{1}{2}$in) at the border.

5 Continue in the same way all round the basket, threading the last pair of ends through the first loop.

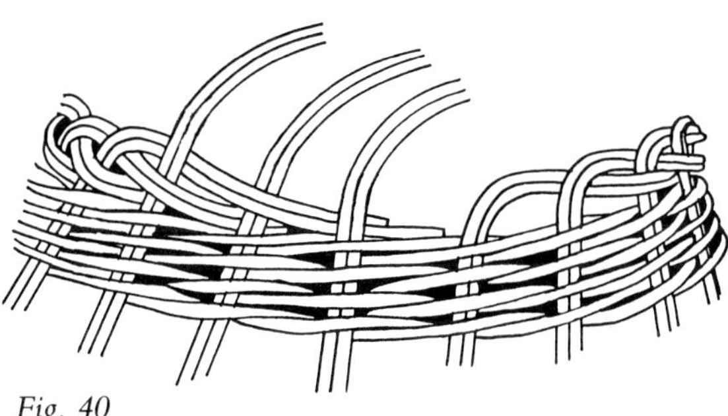
Fig. 40

6 Now pull the ends gently until the loops are all the same height.

Note If you turn the basket upside down on the table, and then look along the surface of the table you will be able to see if any loops need adjusting.

FOOT TRAC

There should be at least 10cm (4in) of stake threaded through to the base for the foot trac.

1 Immerse the long ends in warm water and work the trac.

2 Bend one pair of ends to the right, take them behind the next pair to the right, in front of the next and tuck them behind the third pair.

3 Do the same with the next pair on the right and then work all round the basket until there are three pairs left to weave (fig. 40).

Note Leave the first two loops about 2cm ($\frac{3}{4}$in) high to allow room for the last pairs to be threaded through them.

4 Finish in sequence, threading the last two pairs through the first two loops, and then under the next to the back.

5 Stand the basket on the table to check that it stands firmly. When you are quite satisfied that the foot trac is right turn it upside down and clip the ends with side cutters. Do **not** cut the ends too short. Make sure they rest against a pair of stakes so they won't pop through to the front – leave at least 1cm ($\frac{1}{2}$in) extra to be on the safe side.

BASKET WITH WOODEN BASE

You will need a base with a diameter of approximately 18cm (7in).

1 Cut stakes, one for each hole in the base, from no. 6 cane 33cm (13in) long.

2 Follow the instructions for the Rag Basket for working the foot trac and for waling (the upsett).

3 Cut bye-stakes, one for each stake, 28cm (11in) long and insert them as for the Rag Basket.

4 Now start randing as described on page 33. When using a wooden base, however, there will probably be an uneven number of stakes, so it will not be necessary to work with two lengths of cane as in follow-on randing. Use a single length of no. 3 cane

Fig. 41

and join where necessary. Shape the sides of the basket as shown in colour photo.

5 Wale with no. 6 cane as before.

6 The scalloped border, instead of being brought down over the outside and then threaded through the rows of waling, is simply threaded down into the rows of randing as far as possible (see fig. 41).

TO ADD COLOUR TO THE BASE

Pairing with one length of natural cane and one dyed gives light and dark triangles.

Dyeing cane

It is really very easy to dye cane and gives exciting results.

1 Put one packet of hot water dye in a bucket with a tablespoon of salt.

2 Add a kettle of boiling water. Wearing rubber gloves, place the cane in the solution and swill round until it is the right colour. Add more hot water to cover the cane if necessary.

3 Rinse under the hot tap until the water runs clear, or just leave on newspaper to drain and dry.

The cane can be used straightaway, but wipe on a towel before weaving it into your basket. All dyed cane should be wiped after damping – a quick pull through a cloth is usually enough.

Bleached cane is good for obtaining light colours (yellow for example). It is also less hard on the fingers, turns sharp corners without cracking and sits in place very well, so is useful when building up and doing canework 'tapestry'. It is not quite as strong as the natural unbleached cane however.

Natural dyes

Natural dyes work well. All the following are successful for natural pastel colours: laurel, elder and pyracanthas berries; sweet chestnut shells; onion skins; apple and yew clippings.

PROJECT 3

Mirror with plait border

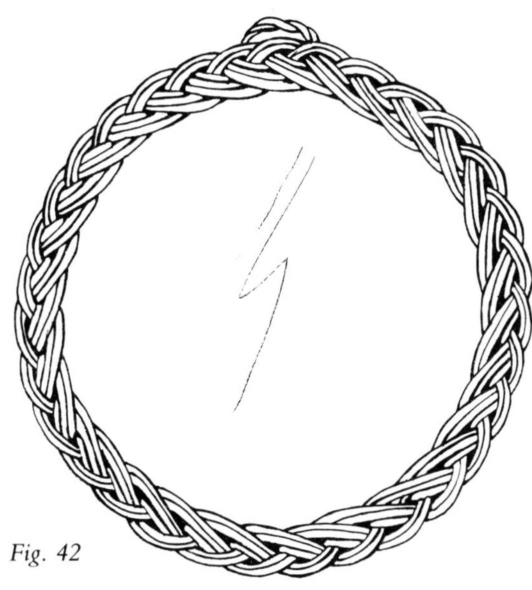
Fig. 42

Last year on a visit to France I bought a mirror like this; it was woven in white willow (fig. 42). It is not difficult to make in cane once you have mastered the plait border, but do be sure you know exactly how to do it before you start. Otherwise it may take too long, and need continual rewetting of the stakes.

MATERIALS

For a mirror with a border diameter of 24cm ($9\frac{1}{2}$in):

- Mirror with 20cm (8in) diameter. This can be obtained from most shops where glass is cut.
- No. 15 cane for base sticks
- Nos. 3 and 6 cane for pairing the base
- No. 6 cane for the side stakes and loop
- No. 8 cane for the three- and four-rod waling
- One small sheet of bubble plastic

Weight of cane used 300g ($10\frac{1}{2}$oz)

METHOD

1 From no. 15 cane cut eight base sticks 25cm (10in) long.

2 Split four of the sticks at the centre and thread the other four through (see page 27).

3 Damp the slath for five minutes in warm water. Damp some no. 3 cane and pair round twice to tie in the slath (see page 28).

4 Open out the slath into **doubles** and pair round for two more rows.

5 Open out into **singles**, continuing to weave round, adjusting the spaces to keep them even.

Note Do not 'crown' the base, keep it flat.

6 After ten or twelve rounds change to no. 6 cane and continue pairing until the base measures exactly the same as the mirror.

7 From no. 6 cane cut 32 side stakes 45cm (18in) long (7cm to insert into the base, 3cm for the side and 35cm for the plait).

8 Slype the ends, damp the stakes so they will not crack when bent up, and insert one firmly down on each side of every base stick (see p.30, paragraph 5).

9 Squeeze with round-nosed pliers (see fig. 33) and bend up each stake. Put an elastic band round to hold the stakes in place.

THE UPSETT

Using no. 8 cane work one round of a four-rod wale (see pages 31–33) followed by two rows of three-rod wale.

Note The finished waling should be just the same height, or a **little** higher, than the surface of the mirror when it is put in place. If it is too high cut a piece of bubble plastic (the kind used for packing) to fit inside, to bring the mirror up to the right height.

This is a good idea anyway as it holds the mirror off the base, which may still be rather damp.

FOUR-PAIR PLAIT BORDER

With the mirror in place and the stakes damp and pliable, work a four-pair plait border. It is almost the same as the three-pair plait on the Doll's Moses basket, except that it has a longer stroke on the inside, thus holding the mirror firmly in place. (For more detailed instructions on how to weave a plait border see pages 77–80).

Note The three-pair plait will work quite well for the mirror border if you prefer. Follow figs. 90–100.

Work the four-pair plait border as for the three-pair plait but adding one extra long stick ('feeder') at the beginning. Follow figs. 90–94.

Then:

1 Add the extra feeder (fig. 43).

2 Take the next pair to the inside. There are now three pairs inside and one pair outside (fig. 44).

3 Bring one pair out over the top of the other two, bending the stake down beside it (fig. 45).

4 Bring one pair outside with one group of three.

Fig. 43

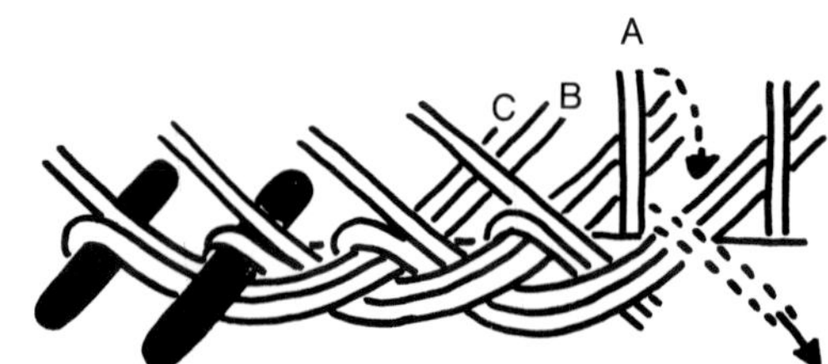

Fig. 44

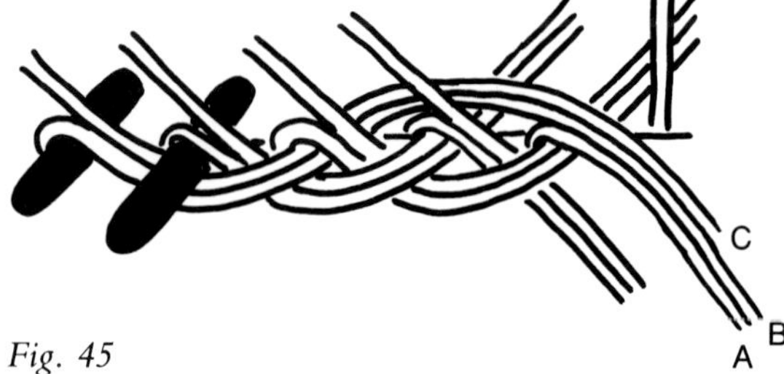

Fig. 45

5 Pick up the **pair** and take it to the inside.

6 Take three pairs inside.

7 Continue plaiting as pages 78–9. The only difference between the three-pair plait and the four-pair plait is that due to the extra feeder there will be **three** pairs on the inside instead of two. Take the first pair (nearest the start) each time, over the top of the other two and out beside the next upright stake, which is bent over with the pair to make another group of three on the outside.

Pitfall As you work the border, pull it inwards towards the mirror. Unless you consciously do this, the border will probably veer away and not hold the mirror tightly. Use a plastic spray bottle filled with water to keep the stakes pliable – nothing looks worse than a plait border with cracked stakes.

Note Do not start the border unless you have the time to finish it all in one go.

FINISHING THE FOUR-PAIR PLAIT

To finish the border work exactly as shown in figs. 98–100. The only difference is that there are four shaded pairs to be woven away (see fig. 100), and four spotted pairs to be woven into the border.

HANGING LOOP

With a length of pliable no. 6 cane, first push a slyped end down beside a stake. Make a loop, pass it under two rows of waling and wind it back round itself. Thread the end away into the weaving. Pull it into the right shape and leave to dry before hanging up. (Fig. 74 shows a handle made in a similar way to this loop).

MIRROR WITH WOODEN BASE

Choose the size of base; to be on the safe side, stake it up and put on two rows of three-rod wale, then measure the space inside before getting the mirror cut.

Most wooden bases have holes drilled 0.5cm ($\frac{1}{4}$in) from the edge. By the time the waling is in place a 17.5cm (7in) base will take a mirror 16cm ($6\frac{1}{4}$in) in diameter.

Check the measurements of your base. The mirror should be cut approximately 1.5cm ($\frac{3}{4}$in) smaller than the base.

1 Count the number of holes and cut the same number of stakes 45cm (18in) long, using no. 6 cane. Work a foot trac (see figs. 3 and 4).

2 With no. 8 cane, weave two or three rows of waling as necessary to bring the top of the waling up to the level of the mirror.

3 Follow the instructions for the plait (see above and pages 38, 77–80).

4 Thread the hanging loop through the waling and at least two stakes.

PROJECT 4

Cheese tray with glass inset

This project is very similar to the Mirror but this time clear glass is used, the base has a decorative weave, a different border is used and a handle added. Mirror glass instead of plain would make hors d'œuvres look wonderful.

MATERIALS

For a tray with a diameter of 26cm ($10\frac{1}{2}$in) and handle height of 20cm (8in):

- A piece of glass 25cm (10in) in diameter and 4mm ($\frac{1}{8}$in) thick, with the edges smoothed off
- No. 15 cane for base sticks
- A small piece of chair cane to decorate the slath (optional)
- No. 3 cane to start pairing the base
- No. 6 cane (natural and two other colours) for spiral waling
- No. 6 cane (natural) for side stakes and waling the edge
- Handle cane 8mm ($\frac{1}{4}$in) thick, approximately 65cm (25in) long
- Glossy lapping cane to wrap the handle

Weight of cane used 400g (14oz)

METHOD

1 From no. 15 cane cut eight base sticks 33cm (13in).

2 Follow the instructions for making the slath as for the Mirror. Decorate the slath if desired with chair cane following fig. 46. Tuck away the ends in the slot in the slath.

3 Pair round as for the Mirror, opening out into doubles and then singles, two rounds of each

4 Cut another stick from the no. 15 cane, 11cm ($4\frac{1}{2}$in) long. Slype one end. This is going to provide another base stick to make the number 17.

Note In order to weave a spiral wale in three different colours the number of base sticks (or if the pattern was being woven on the side of a basket, the number of side stakes) must be divisible by the number of weavers plus two. Some other variations created by colour, weaves and numbers of stakes can be found at the end of the chapter.

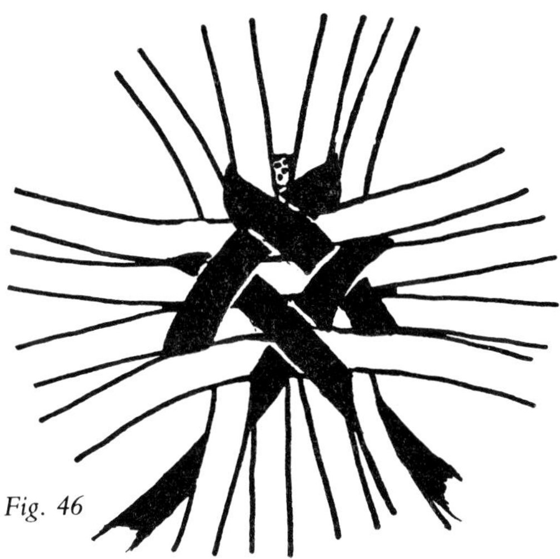
Fig. 46

5 Select a space (perhaps one is larger than the others) and push the new stick into the pairing beside another stick.

SPIRAL WALING

1 Choose the colours. I used brown, a darkish yellow and natural. Work a three-rod wale (see pages 15–16) pressing well down with your fingers and adjusting the spaces, especially where the new stake was added, to make the gaps equal.

Note There is no need to change the stroke in spiral waling.

2 Work on a clean, flat surface. After about five rows, if you would like to reverse the direction of the spiral, cut the ends off and leave them at the back.

3 Now weave anti-clockwise. Put the three colours in the spaces where they ended, but reverse the wale from right to left, taking C across B and A (see the cover photo).

4 Continue with this change of direction, keeping the base flat all the time. When the base measures the same size as the glass, finish, fastening the ends with a clothes peg.

STAKING UP AND WALING

1 Cut 34 stakes from no. 6 cane, 46cm (18in) long. Slype and insert one on either side of each base stick.

2 Check the size of the base with the glass again. If it is not quite the same size put on another round or two of waling.

3 Prick up the stakes and tie with string or a rubber band.

4 Using two full lengths of damp no. 6 cane work a four-rod wale round the base followed by a row of three-rod. Follow instructions on pages 31–33 (figs. 34–35).

5 Insert the glass and work another row of three-rod. Remove the tie and work two more final rows, upsetting the sides so they are quite straight.

ROPE BORDER

1 Add a handle liner on each side of the tray as for the Rag Basket. This border is very tight, so you will not be able to insert the handle later unless a space has been made by the liner.

2 Slype six pieces of no. 6 cane 35cm (14in) long. Push them well down into the waling on the right-hand side of three consecutive stakes, two to each stake. Place the first two beside the stake to the left of the handle liner.

3 Soak the ends of all the stakes in warm water, for at least five minutes.

4 Hold the first group of three stakes (the first two added plus the original stake beside them) firmly in your right hand. Twist them tightly in a clockwise direction about three times and bring them down to the front of the basket, being careful not to let them untwist.

5 Take the twist in front of the next two

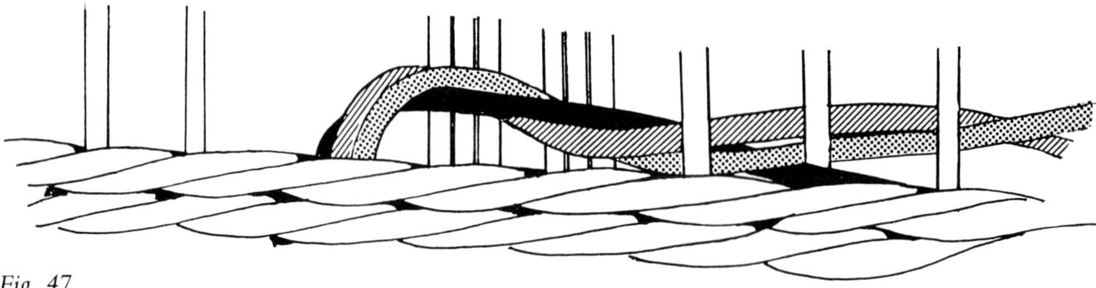

Fig. 47

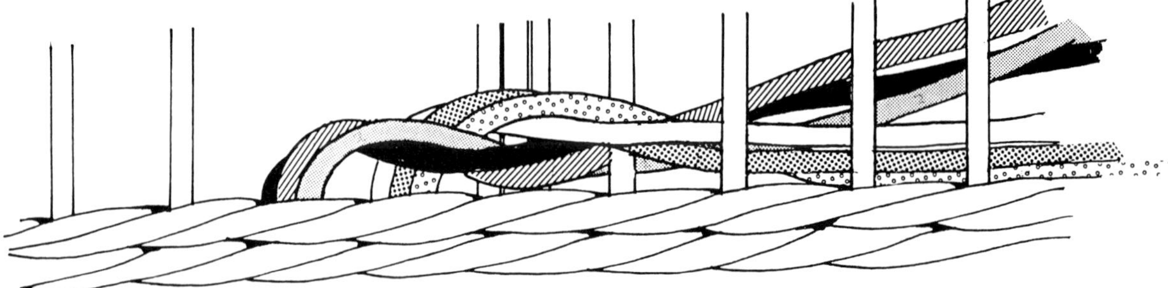

Fig. 48

groups of three to the right and through to the back where they will rest (fig. 47).

Note These ends should now be held by one hand so they remain tightly twisted while the next group of three is twisted and taken across the next four stakes (one group of three and a single) (fig. 48).

6 Twist the third group of three tightly, take it across two stakes and leave it at the back.

7 The next and subsequent moves consist of picking up the two longest stakes from the left-hand twist (leaving behind the one that is under the other two) and twisting them together with the next single stake, as above. Continue round to the start.

Note As you reach the handle liners, negotiate them carefully, keeping the twist tight and deciding whether to take all or just some of the stakes in front of the liner.

8 When the last twist is threaded to the inside, redamp the border if it has dried out. Carefully remove the six extra stakes one at a time while threading away two from each of the last groups (also one at a time), following the pathway of each cane as it is extracted.

HANDLE

1 Cut a piece of handle cane 60cm (24in) long. Soak it for five minutes and slype the ends to form a long gradual point. Bend the handle gently over your knee to obtain the right curve, remove the liners and put the handle in place.

2 Take a long length of glossy lapping cane, soak it, slype one end and push it down into the border and the waling on the left-hand side of one end of the handle.

3 Take the long end diagonally across the

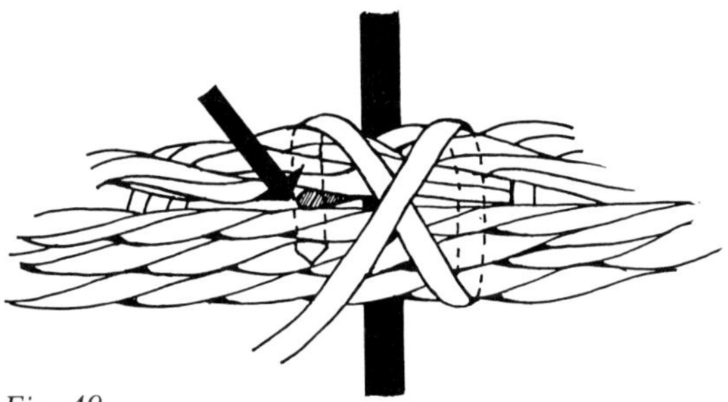

Fig. 49

front from left to right, under three rows of waling to the inside, up and over the border to the right of the handle, diagonally across to the left, through the waling and up, then over the border to repeat the first two crossings again (fig. 49).

4 Cut two lengths of coloured no. 6 cane (to match the ones used in the base) the same length as the handle. They will lie on top of the handle along its length. Wrap the lapping cane three times around the handle and the ends of the coloured canes to hold them in place.

5 Continue to wrap tightly over the handle, twice over the coloured canes and twice under, until the end is reached.

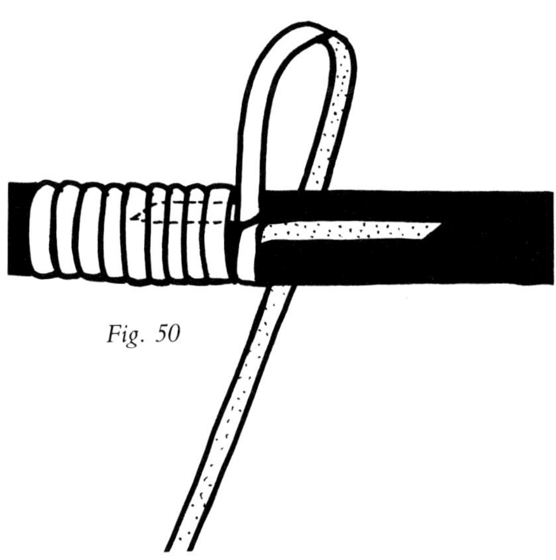

Fig. 50

6 Repeat the crossover as in step 3, and weave the end away into the waling.

Joining

As shown in the diagram below, wrap in a new length of lapping cane on the underside of the handle at least four times before it changes place with the old end. Hammer the join gently to flatten afterwards (fig. 50).

PEGGING THE HANDLE

Follow the instructions given for the Rag Basket (see fig. 49 – the arrow points to the peg).

COLOUR VARIATIONS

Three-rod wale

A Three weavers in different colours, woven over a number of stakes divisible by three, will produce three vertical stripes.

B Three weavers, one coloured and two natural, woven over a number of stakes divisible by three plus one, will produce a spiral inside the basket and a variegated pattern outside.

C Three weaves in different colours, woven over a number of stakes divisible by three plus two (as for the Cheese Tray), will produce a spiral on the outside and variegation on the inside.

Pairing

A One plain and one coloured weaver over an even number of stakes will produce stripes.

B One plain and one coloured weaver over an uneven number of stakes will produce a spiral.

PROJECT 5

Madeira platter

I was visiting my Aunt Trudi in Switzerland a few years ago. At breakfast she served up the toast on a delightful little platter. 'Where did you get this?' I asked admiringly. 'You gave it to me', she laughed. Apparently I had made it during my occupational therapy training in 1956 and had forgotten all about it! The platter is illustrated here in two different sizes – instructions are given for both.

MATERIALS

For a platter with a diameter of 24cm (9½in):

- No. 8 cane for the stakes
- No. 6 cane for the pairing
- No. 6 cane (dyed brown) for the waling (for dyeing instructions see page 36)

Weight of platter approximately 90g (3oz)

For a platter with a diameter of 16cm (6½in):

- No. 3 cane throughout

Weight of platter approximately 30g (1oz)

METHOD

These instructions are for the larger platter. Those for the smaller platter are at the end of the chapter.

1 From no. 8 cane cut 16 stakes 1m (40in) long.

2 Soak the stakes in warm water for about five minutes.

3 Pierce one group of four stakes (slightly off centre) and thread them onto a bodkin. Do the same with the other three groups of four.

4 With the help of a bodkin thread the four groups through each other (fig. 51).

5 When all the sticks are threaded gradually ease them together to form the slath.

6 Soak a piece of no. 6 cane until it is really pliable. In order to bend it sharply without it cracking follow the instructions given in step 2 of 'Tying in the slath', page 28.

TYING IN THE SLATH (PAIRING)

1 Loop the bent length of cane round one group of stakes and pair twice round the eight groups of four stakes (fig. 52).

Note For a definition of pairing and the method of tying in a slath with pairing see page 28, but note that in this project the

Fig. 51

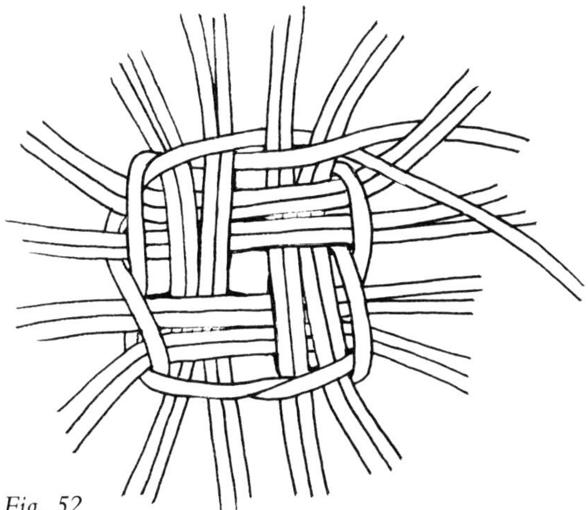
Fig. 52

opening out of the stakes is different, as described below.

2 Damp the slath and continue pairing opening out the groups of four stakes into pairs.

3 Work carefully and firmly; the base should have a slight but not too pronounced crown (see page 29).

4 When the base measures 14cm ($5\frac{1}{2}$in) after about 12 rows tuck the ends under the last row and cut off, leaving ends of at least 1cm $\frac{1}{2}$in).

BYE-STAKES

Using no. 8 cane cut 32 bye-stakes 40cm (16in) long. Point them at one end and insert two firmly between each pair of stakes, pushing them through the pairing right up to the slath.

WALING

1 Damp four lengths of no. 6 dyed cane about 1m (40in) long. Draw them through a length of old towel to remove any 'loose' colour.

2 With the concave side of the platter towards you insert the four lengths between four consecutive stakes.

3 Start working a four-rod wale (in front of three and behind one) round the base, separating the stakes into singles. Push the cane down between each stake with the point of a bodkin to make the waling sit tight upon the top of the pairing.

4 After just one row finish as in figs. 15–17.

MADEIRA BORDER

1 Damp the ends of the stakes, but try not to wet the coloured waling in case it runs. Regroup the stakes into fours.

2 With the concave side facing you take one group of four stakes and make a loop about 6cm ($2\frac{1}{2}$in) above the waling. Weave behind the next group of four to the right, in front of the next, behind the next, in front of the next and tuck the end behind the fifth group (fig. 53).

3 Now weave the next group to the right in the same way.

Fig. 53

4 Continue round the basket working the border until the last four groups of stakes are left.

5 In order to make the connection perfect at the end, damp the beginning of the border and undo the first four groups of stakes so they stand upright again. Now work the last eight groups of stakes in and out of each other to match the part already completed.

FOOT TRAC

1 Damp the unwoven ends if they have dried out.

2 Weave each group behind the group to its right and leave the ends outside.

3 To finish, tuck the last group under the first loop.

4 Give each group a firm pull to make sure it is secure and trim the ends carefully.

SMALLER PLATTER

The smaller platter differs slightly in the construction of the slath. The stakes are **laid** across each other instead of pierced.

- No. 3 cane is used throughout.
- The length of the stakes is 76cm (30in).
- The length of the bye-stakes is 33cm (13in).
- Three-rod waling is used instead of four-rod.
- The Madeira border and foot trac are the same.

PROJECT 6

Cane and willow bread basket

The side of this basket was made using willows grown in my garden. The colours are the natural colours of the bark. I used the willow about three weeks after it had been cut in February while it was still pliable.

Other garden or hedgerow materials could have been used just as well (see the notes at the end of the book). Coloured cane, plastic packing tape, or 0.5cm wide strips of coloured cardboard (varnished afterwards) could be used in the same way for the French randing.

Alternatively work the side in no. 3 cane, using slewing (see Note, page 95) or follow-on randing (see page 33).

MATERIALS

For a basket with a base diameter of 20cm (8in), top diameter of 24cm ($9\frac{1}{2}$in) and side height of 10cm (4in):

- No. 12 or 14 cane for the bottom sticks
- No. 6 cane for pairing the base, the upsett and wrapping the handles
- No. 8 cane for the side stakes and top waling
- No. 12 cane for the bye-stakes
- No. 15 cane for the handle bows
- 24 pieces of willow (with another 24 handy in case required), about 30–50cm (12–20in) long and not more than 0.5cm ($\frac{1}{4}$in) thick at the butt end, for the French randing (fig. 54)

Weight of basket 220g (8oz), about half cane and half willow

METHOD

1 Cut six base sticks from no. 12 or 14 cane 24cm ($9\frac{1}{2}$in) long.

2 Follow the instructions for making a woven base (see pages 26–30), finishing pairing when the diameter measures 18cm (7in).

3 Cut 24 side stakes from no. 8 cane, 40cm (16in) long. Point one end, soak in warm water for about five minutes and stake up following the instructions on pages 30–31, but this time using one stake only on either side of each bottom stick (see fig. 32).

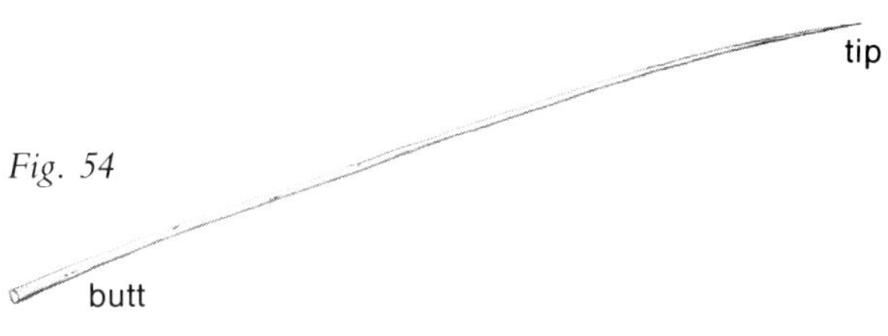

Fig. 54

4 Using no. 6 cane work one round of a four-rod wale and then three rounds of three-rod (see pages 31–33).

BYE-STAKES

Using no. 12 cane cut 24 bye-stakes 10cm (4in) long (the height required for the basket). Point one end of each and push down on the right-hand side of each stake, being careful that the pointed ends do not go through the bottom of the basket.

Pitfall Do not be tempted to omit the bye-stakes. No. 8 stakes by themselves will not be strong enough to give the basket a good shape. Extra-strong bye-stakes are needed to withstand the pressure of the willow.

Redamp the stakes if they have become dry and gently press outwards.

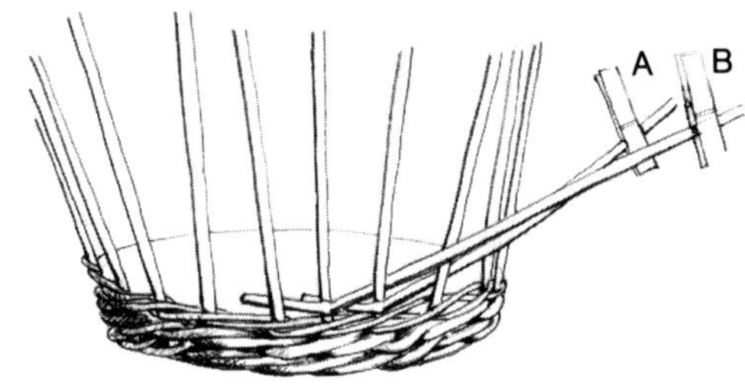

Fig. 55

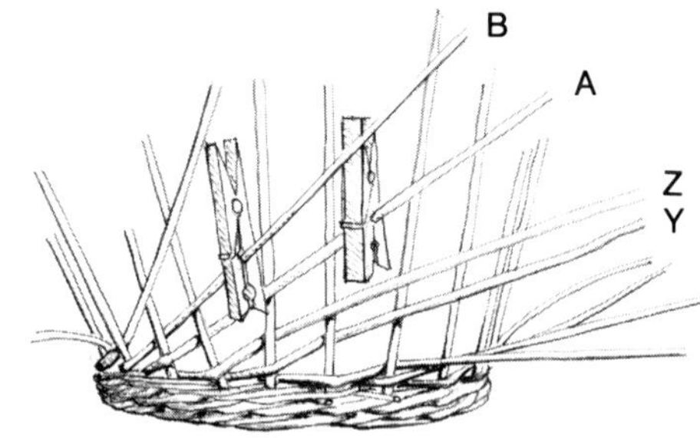

Fig. 56

STARTING FRENCH RANDING

This form of randing is used in willow basketmaking where the material is thicker at one end than the other see fig. 54).

1 Select 24 rods of equal thickness. Trim the thick (or 'butt') end so all the rods are the same length.

2 Insert the butt end of the first rod, A, in between two stakes. Weave it to the right, in front of the next stake, behind the next, and leave it at the front.

3 Insert a second rod, B, in the same way, one space to the **left**. Weave it in front of the next to the right, behind the next and leave it at the front.

As you will see, rod B is lying on top of rod A (fig. 55).

4 Mark these two rods with a clothes peg on each.

5 Continue inserting butts to the left (turning the basket anti-clockwise as you work) until the marked rods are reached and you have two more rods to insert, numbers 23 and 24.

6 Gently lift up the tips of the marked rods and insert the last two in place. First Y, weaving it to the right exactly like all the others.

7 Place the second rod, Z, in the remaining space under A. This last rod is also woven to the right in the same manner as all the rest (fig. 56).

8 Push the marked rods back into place. There should now be 24 rods fanning out from the side of the basket, one for each side stake (one emerging from each space).

Note If you find you have missed one out, look inside to see where the butt should lie, lift the rod immediately above this space, insert the butt and weave the rod to the right in sequence with the others.

CONTINUING FRENCH RANDING

1 To start the second round of French randing weave the right-hand marked rod (A) to the right, in front of one, behind one and out to the front.

2 Do the same with the left-hand marked rod (B) as in fig. 57.

3 You will see that these two rods are now lying parallel to two other rods (Y and Z in the previous row). Peg these two pairs together. You have created two spaces to the left, (see arrows), so that all the rest of the rods in the second row will have a space to lie in as they are woven to the right.
Note Waling is not shown in fig. 57 for clarity.

4 Continue to weave the rods in sequence as for the first row, until you reach the two pairs of marked rods.

Note In these two pairs, the rods underneath (Y and Z) have not yet been woven into the second round of randing.

5 Lift up the top two marked rods (A and B). Weave Y first (the one under A) then Z (the one under B).

6 Press the marked rods back into place. You will see that the second row is now complete and that there is a rod in every space, so you are now ready to weave the third row in exactly the same way.

7 Continue weaving complete rows, compressing one upon the other with your fingers as you work to avoid any gaps between rows. When the shortest rod has been woven to its tip, finish the row and leave all the ends outside.

Note If you have made a mistake and two rods are coming out from one space, (not the marked ones where doubling up is deliberate) raise the top one and weave away the one underneath.

8 If the 24 rods you have just used are fairly short – mine were around 38cm (15in) – you can now add another 24 on top of the first exactly the same way as you started. Work them out to their tips.

9 Tap down the rows gently with a rapping iron to get them close and even.

WALING

Using no. 8 cane weave three rows of a three-rod wale to give strength to the top of the basket. Remember to change the stroke at the end of each row and finish correctly. Tap down the waling so the edge of the basket is the same height all the way round.

Fig. 57

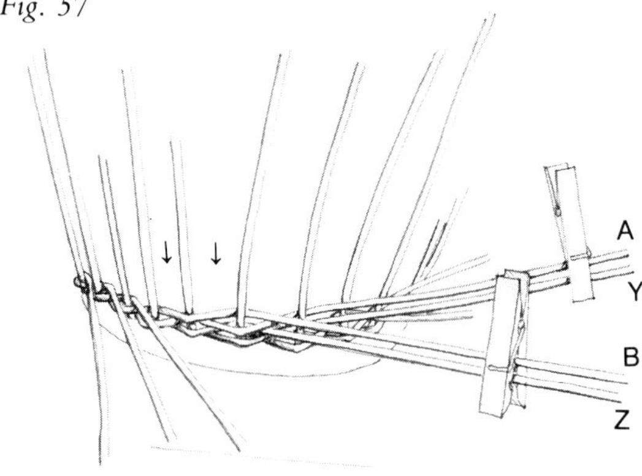

THREE-ROD PLAIN BORDER

This is a strong border and is started by taking three rods down behind their neighbours to the right. (Other borders may, like waling, be four-, five- or six-rod).

1 Soak the stakes from their tips down to and including the top edge of the waling. They must be really pliable so test the tips (see page 00) of one or two of the stakes to see if they can be easily bent at a right angle.

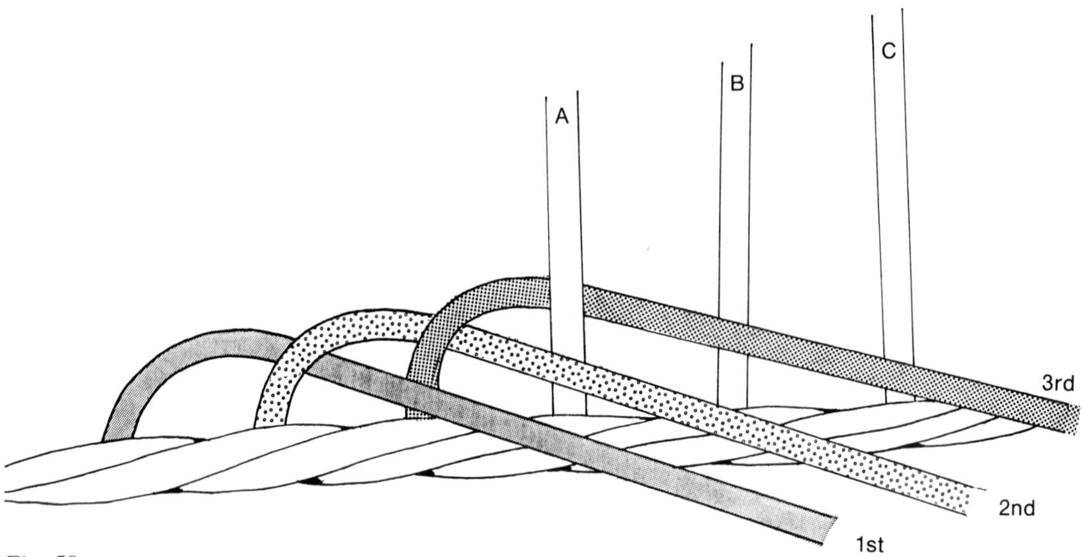

Fig. 58

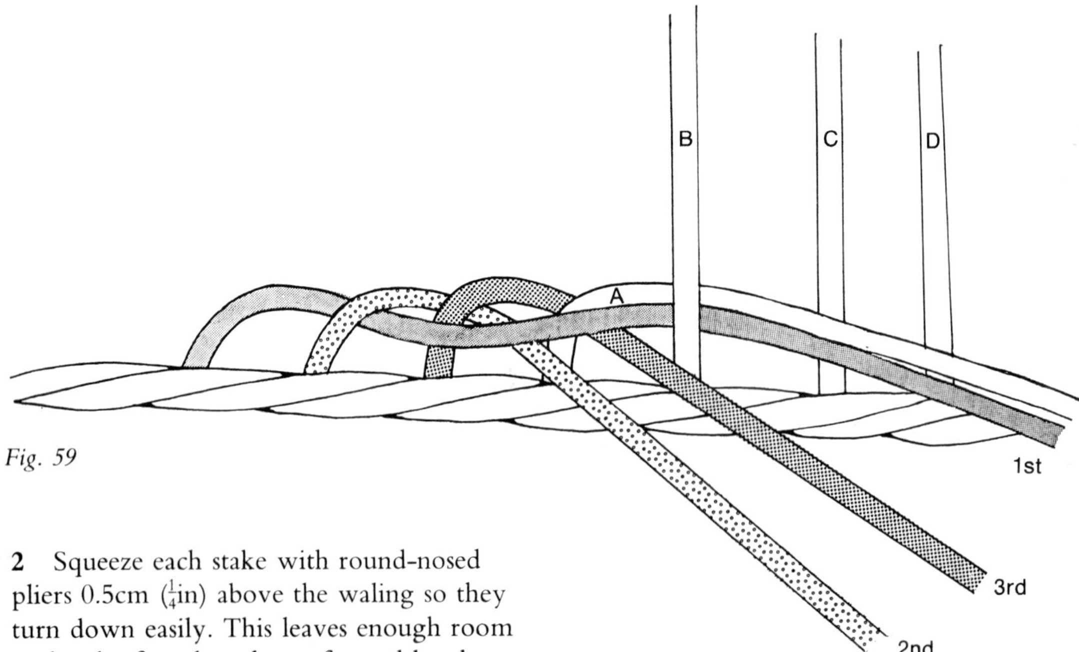

Fig. 59

2 Squeeze each stake with round-nosed pliers 0.5cm ($\frac{1}{4}$in) above the waling so they turn down easily. This leaves enough room under the first three loops formed by the border to thread away the last three ends.

3 Bend one stake down behind the stake to its right and bring it out to the front. Do the same with the second and the third. Now you have the three rods ready to start the three-rod border (fig. 58).

4 Take the first rod which was bent over in front of the next upright stake to its right (A) behind the next (B) and out to the front (fig. 59).

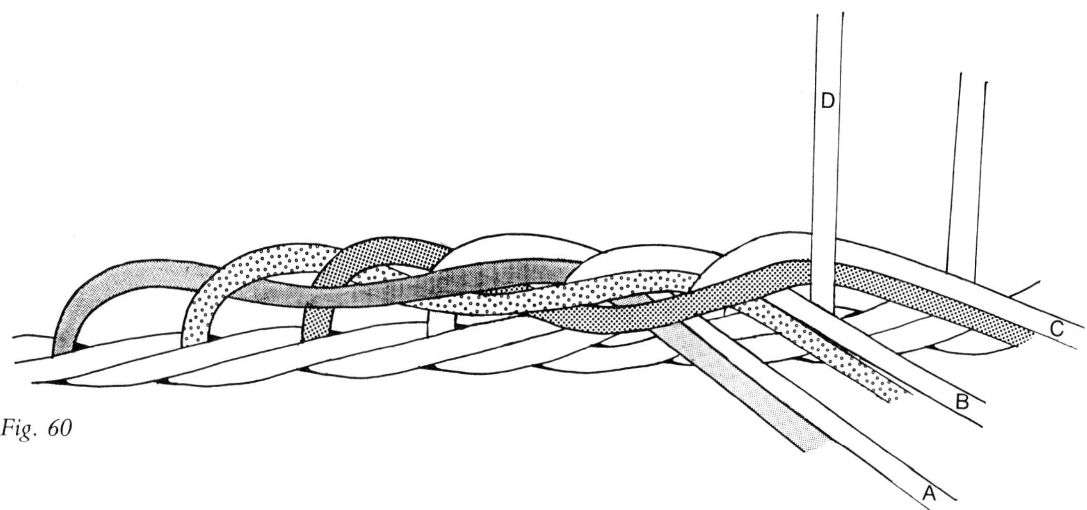

Fig. 60

Stake A is then brought down beside the first and **behind** it, firmly down on the top edge of the basket.

Note These pairs of stakes should, throughout the border, lie side by side firmly down on the top of the waling.

5 The second stake is now taken in front of one (B) behind one (C), and the upright stake (B) comes down beside and behind it.

6 Now take the third stake in front of one and behind one in the same manner, bringing the upright stake beside and behind it (so they are firmly side by side). There are now three pairs, instead of three singles (fig. 60).

7 Counting the pairs of stakes (from furthest right), take the fifth stake (marked A – the longest of the third pair from the right). Weave it in front of one, behind one and bring the next upright one beside and behind it, as above. This leaves one stake as a single (the sixth) and creates another pair furthest right. Continue round the basket,

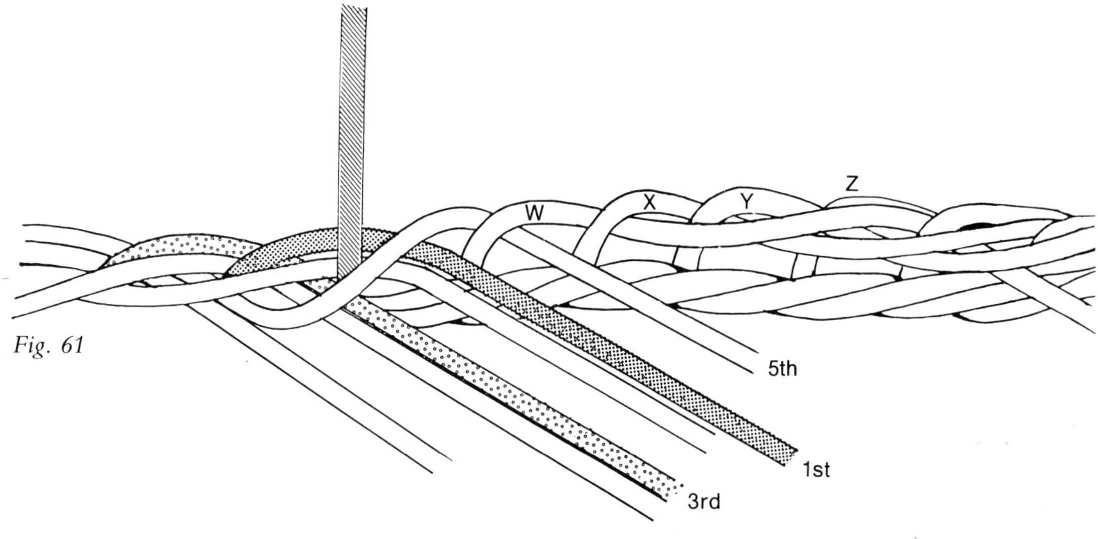

Fig. 61

taking the fifth stake each time (the longest rod of the pair on the left), in front of one, etc., as before. The second rod of the third pair is left, and woven away or cut off afterwards.

Pitfall It is most important to see that the 'upright' stake, when it is brought down, lies **behind**. If it crosses to the front of its pair, the wrong stake may be used in step 7, and the border may come undone later when the ends are trimmed.

8 Continue round the basket working the border as in step 7. When you reach the first stakes you turned down, and there is only one still standing, take the fifth stake in front of this upright, behind W and through the loop to the front (fig. 61).

The upright stake is brought down beside it (behind it) and out to the front under W. This stake now becomes the first (fig. 62).

FINISHING THE THREE-ROD BORDER

1 Take the fifth stake (longest of the pair on the left) beside and in front of the first stake bent over (W), under the next (X) and out to the front. So it comes out under **one** stake (fig. 63).

2 There are now two pairs left. Take the third (the longest of the left-hand pair) alongside the next single stake to the right (X), then under Y and W and out to the front. So it comes out under **two** (fig. 64).

3 There is now just one pair left. Take the longer one (which lies to the right), alongside Y, behind Z and under **three** (Z and the ends of W and X) and out to the front (fig. 65).

So when weaving away the last three ends:

- The first lies under one stake
- The second lies under two stakes
- The third lies under three stakes

Now each stake can be cut off close to the edge to finish the border neatly. Alternatively, if they are long enough, weave a follow-on trac. This gives a neat appearance as there are no ends on the outside.

Fig. 62

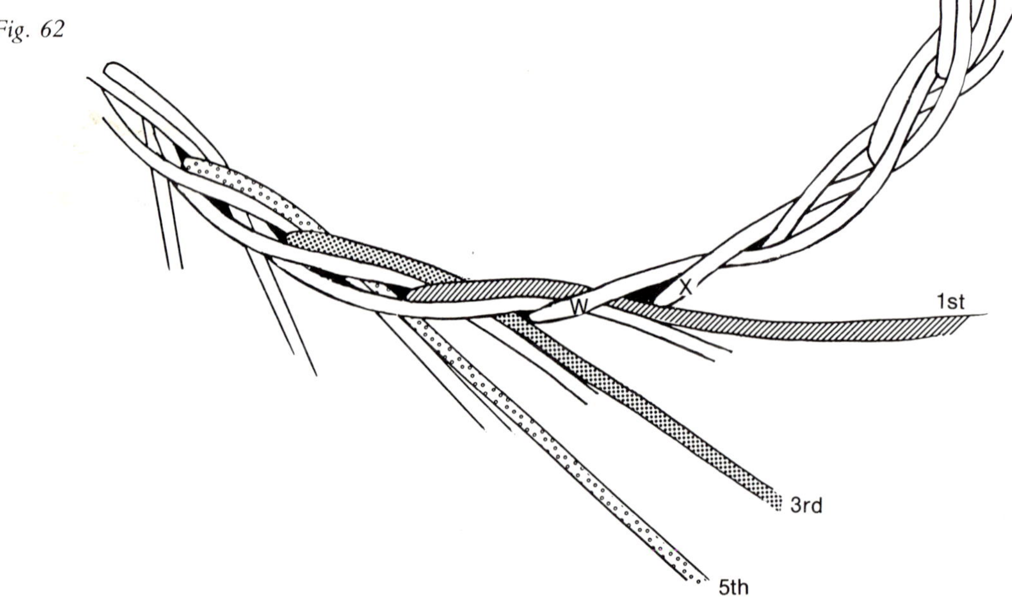

Fig. 63

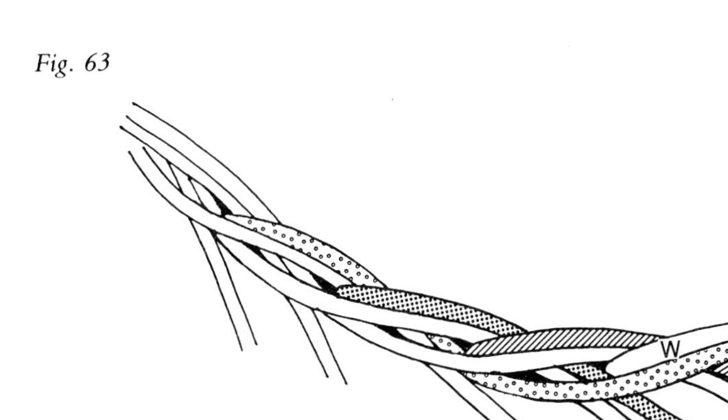

Fig. 64

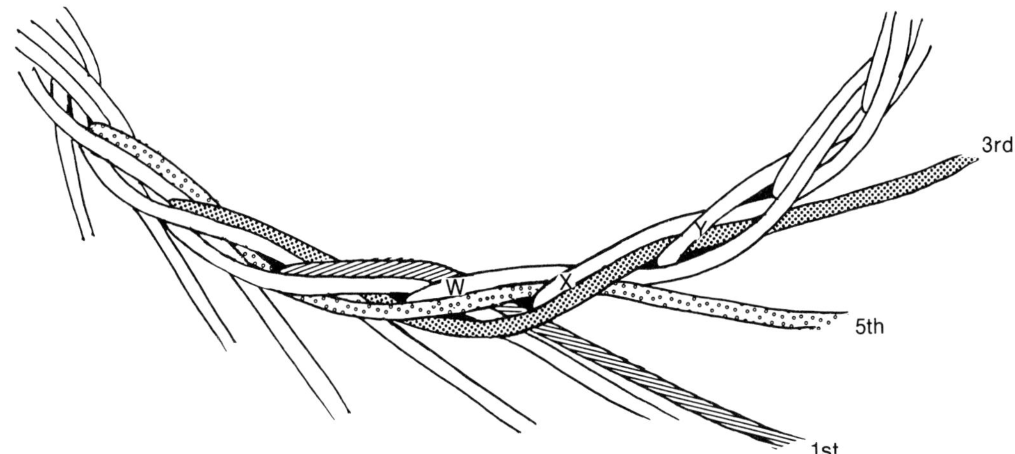

Fig. 65

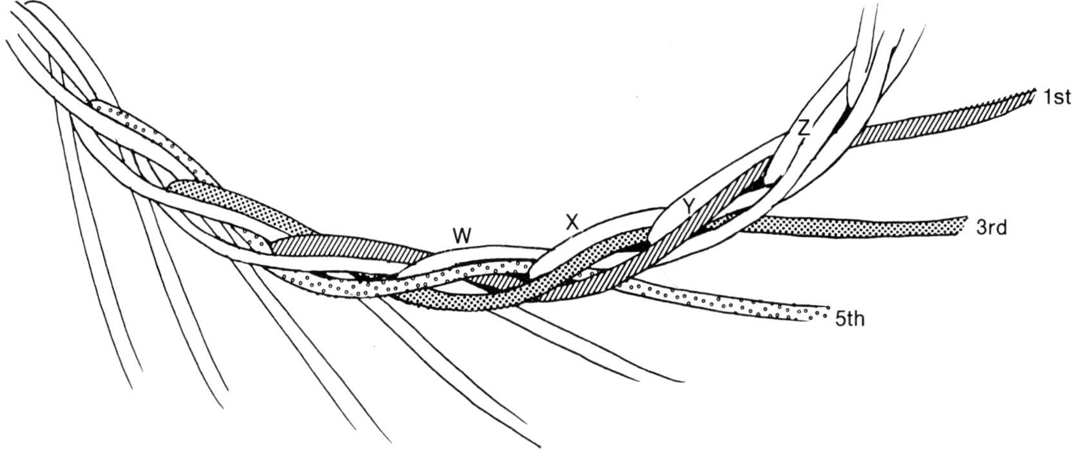

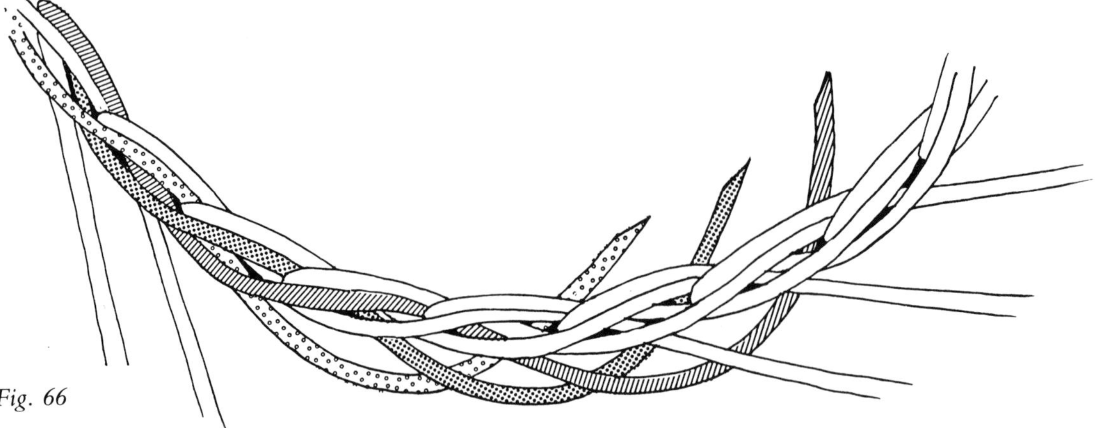

Fig. 66

FOLLOW-ON TRAC

There should be at least 8 to 10cm (3–4in) of stake left in order to weave the follow-on trac.

1 Cut the end of each stake to a point. Pick up any one and, holding the basket on its side, pass this stake under the next two and, lifting the second one, push the end of the stake inside between the border and the waling where it will rest against the back of the next stake (fig. 66).

2 Work around the border in this way and cut off the ends neatly.

Pitfall Be very careful not to cut the ends so short that they pop through to the outside. They must rest against a stake on the inside of the basket.

HANDLES

1 Cut two pieces of no. 15 for the handles. They should be long enough to reach down through the top waling. Allow a depth of two fingers under the loop and cover a distance of four stakes – the ends of the bow are inserted beside two side stakes with two stakes between (fig. 67).

2 Slype the ends of both handles, making sure the bows are exactly the same length. Damp and shape them, then push them down beside the appropriate stakes.

WRAPPING THE HANDLES

1 Damp a length of no. 6 cane 14 times the length of the handle bow. Slype the end, and holding the basket between your knees work on the bow on the far side.

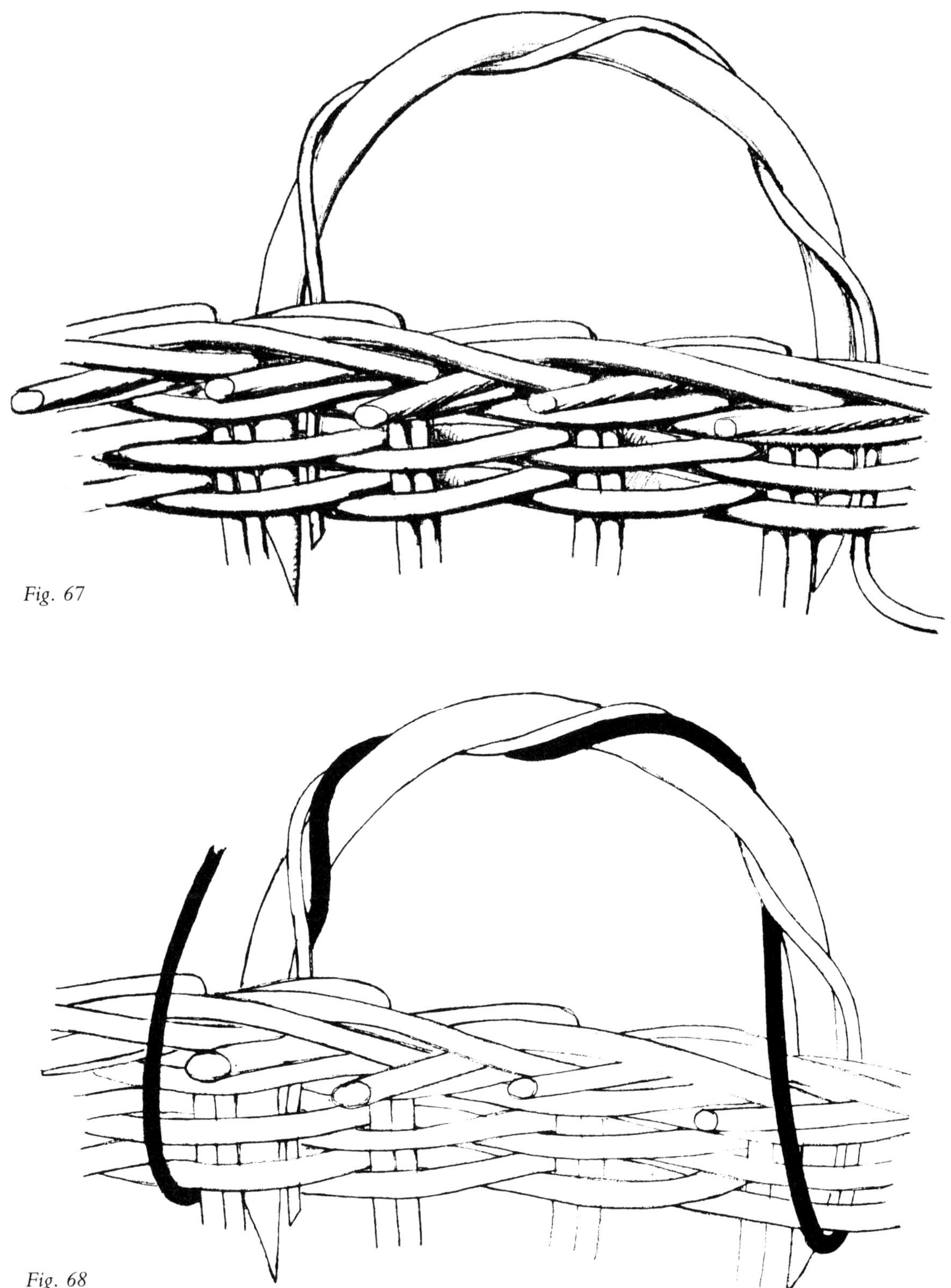

Fig. 67

Fig. 68

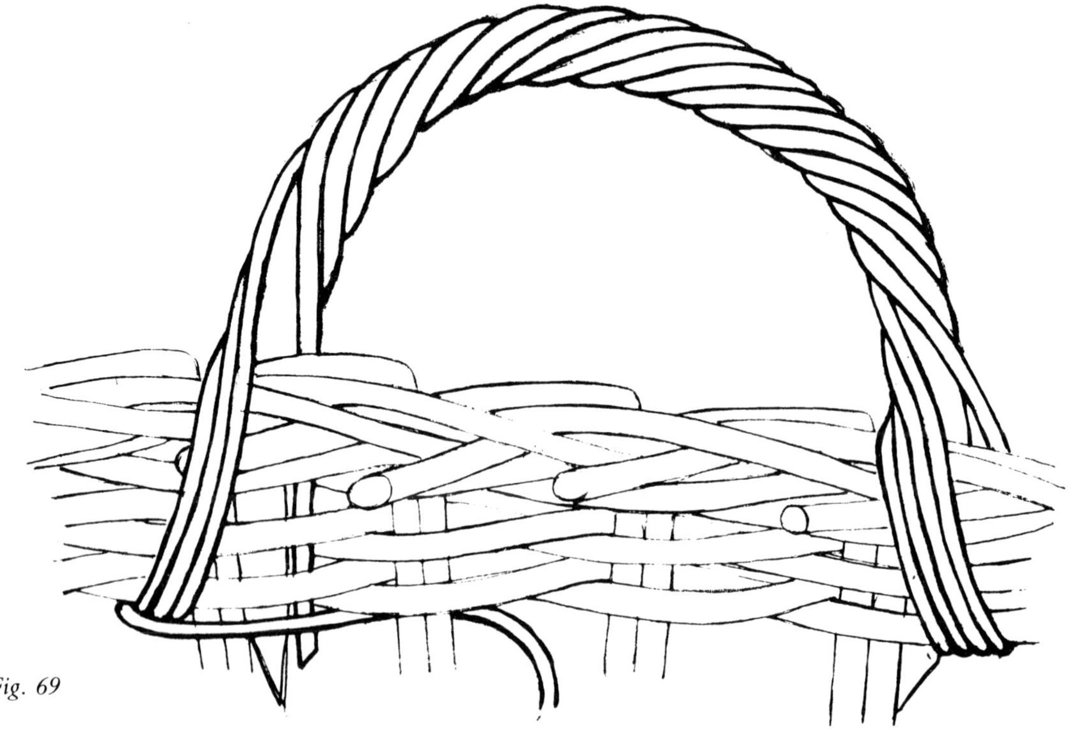

Fig. 69

2 Push the slyped end of the no. 6 cane down into the waling under the bow on the left (fig. 67).

3 Bring the cane under the bow to the **inside** up and over the bow three times.

4 Take the cane over the border to the outside of the basket. Make a gap with a bodkin underneath the waling to the right of the handle bow and pass the cane through to the inside.

5 The second wrap starts by going under the bow to the outside and then follows up over the bow beside the first wrap. It wraps twice over the bow (see fig. 68).

6 Take the cane outside, to the left of the handle bow, and pass it under the waling to the inside.

7 The third wrap winds back over the bow on the other side of the first strand.

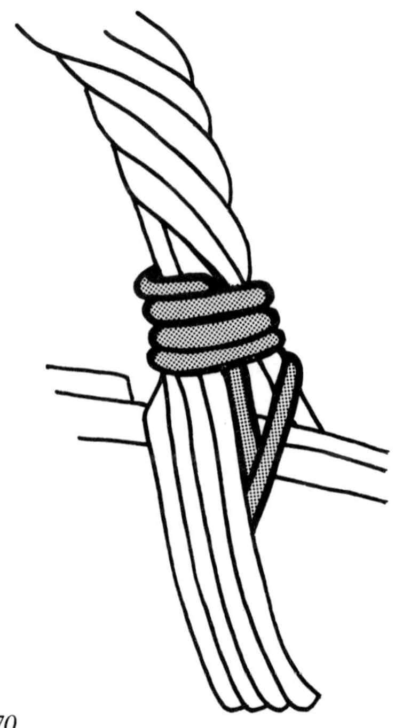

Fig. 70

Then thread it under the waling from the outside to the inside (on the right).

8 Wrap the handle four more times to fill the gaps, the fourth wrap lying beside the second, the fifth beside the third, the sixth beside the fourth and the seventh beside the fifth. This may **sound** complicated, but it falls into place quite naturally as long as its started correctly at the beginning.

9 Thread the last end away under the bow from the outside and weave it away into the side of the basket (fig. 69).

10 You can wrap the ends of the handle if you like, as shown (fig. 70).

PROJECT 7

Self-locking tray

Easy to make and amazingly strong if made with substantial material, this tray can be made with colourful hedgerow twigs, garden prunings, willow, cane, etc. We made 20 of them for my daughter Olivia's wedding reception and they looked lovely.

These instructions are for cane; I used handle cane – 8mm ($\frac{5}{16}$in) thick. It could be made with smaller sizes of cane, but should be scaled down accordingly.

MATERIALS

For a tray with a diameter of 33cm (13in):

- One full length of handle cane (approximately 3m (10ft)) for the twisted ring

Fig. 71

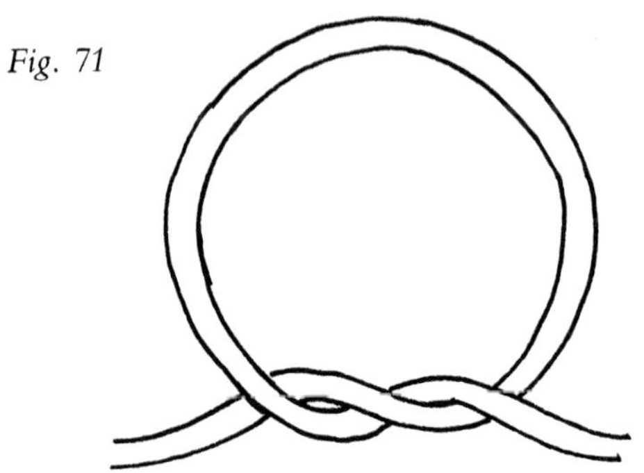

- Enough lengths of handle cane to fill the diameter of the circle, side by side (approximately 300g (11oz))
- No. 12, 14 or 15 cane (about 6m (21ft)) for the tension sticks
- No. 11 or 12 cane for the small, twisted handles

Weight of tray 325g (12oz)

METHOD

Dye the cane if required following the instructions on page 36.

Note The cane must be straight for this tray. See the note on page 13 on straightening out curved cane.

1 Find a rigid round container with the required diameter of the tray.

2 Soak the 3m (10ft) length of handle cane in warm water for ten minutes and make it into a ring (fig. 71).

3 Fit it around the container to get the right size, making sure that both the ends are the same length. Then carefully remove it, keeping the size unaltered. Wind each end twice round the ring and overlap 20cm (8in) (fig. 72).

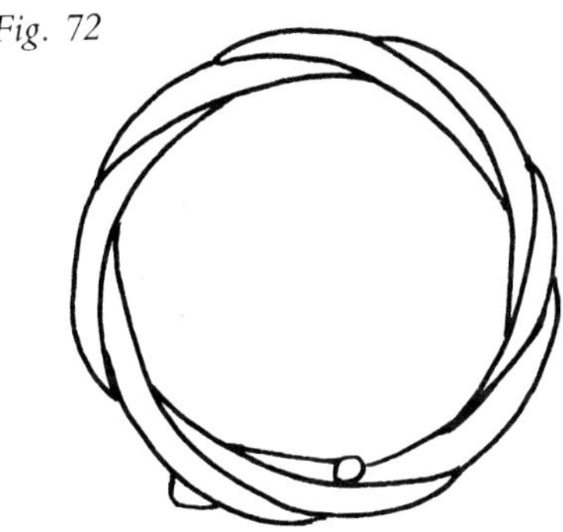
Fig. 72

4 Force the ring back over the container (it should fit tightly) and leave overnight to dry out and set.

WEAVING THE TRAY

1 The next day cut ten pieces of no. 12, 14 or 15 cane the diameter of the ring plus 10cm (4in). Lay these across the circle in two groups of five, dividing the ring into thirds. These will be the tension sticks (see the colour photo).

2 Cut three pieces of handle cane, dyed blue, at least 10cm (4in) longer than the diameter of the circle.

3 Slip the first piece of handle cane into position across the centre of the ring, under the left-hand edge, over one group of five tension sticks, under the next and rest the end over the right-hand edge of the ring.

4 Now slip another blue cane under the right-hand edge of the ring, beside the middle stick. Weave it over one group of tension sticks, then slide it sideways under the second group and rest it on the left-hand edge of the ring beside the middle stick.

5 Turn the tray 180° and weave in another blue cane on the other side of the middle stick, under the ring, then over the group of tension sticks. Slip it under the next group and rest it on the edge of the ring.

Note It is easier to work on the far side of the middle stick, turning the tray as each new stick is added. (The middle stick should be in a horizontal position.) It is tricky getting the first three sticks in place, but once that is achieved you will find they are held in place by tension and adding the rest is easy.

Check that the first cane is exactly in the middle and at a right angle to the groups of five tension sticks.

6 Continue to build up the tray, always adding one cane at a time on either side of the centre. Keep pressing the tray at the sides to prevent it becoming oval.

Note Always slip the end of the new stick **under** the edge of the ring **first**. Then weave it over a group of five, slip it sideways under the next group and over the ring at the edge. This is much easier, especially as the tension increases.

7 When you have a gap of approximately 3cm ($1\frac{1}{4}$in) left at either side, it will be necessary to cut the outside of each group of five sticks, so there is room to weave in the next stick (see fig. 73).

8 Repeat this before weaving in the next stick.

Note The last two or three pieces of cane to be woven in on each side will need to be a little thinner than the handle cane.

SMALL TWISTED HANDLES

1 Cut two pieces of thick cane, no. 11 or 12, about 1m (40in) long. Soak them in warm water for about ten minutes.

2 Slype one end of each. Take one and drive it about 8cm (3in) into one of the groups of tension sticks.

3 Hold the tray on your lap and work on the side furthest from you.

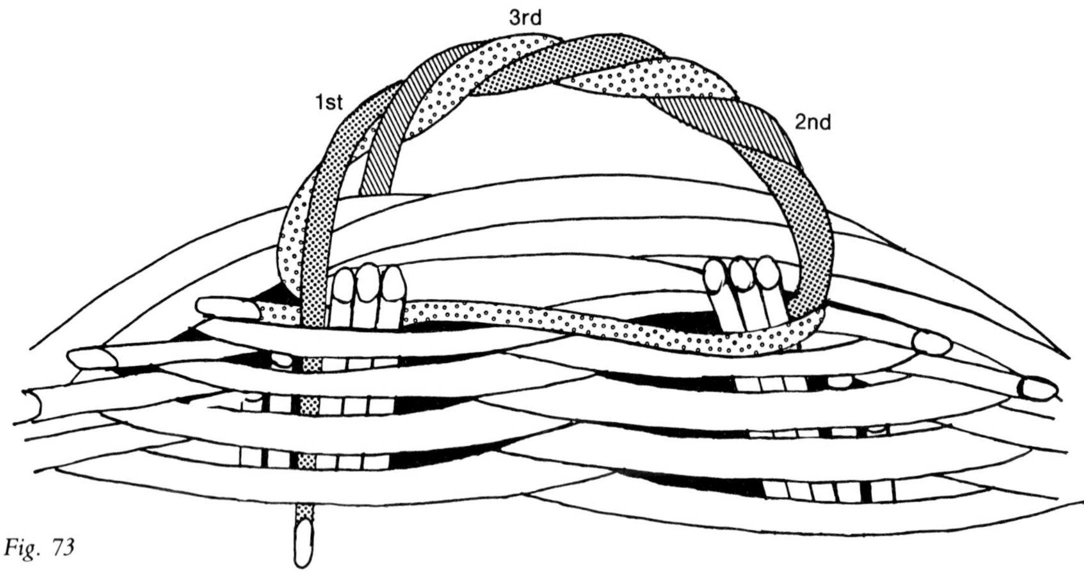

Fig. 73

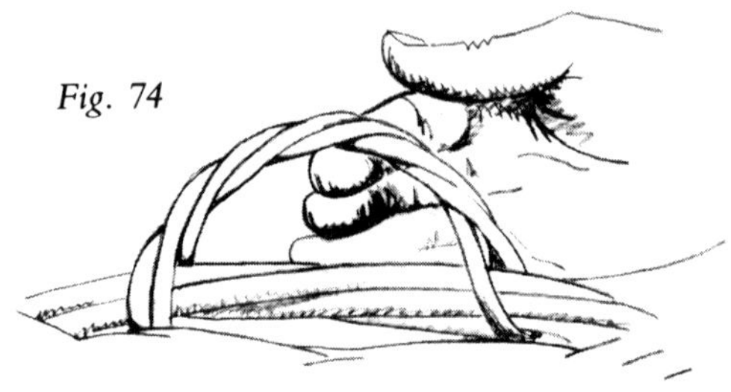

Fig. 74

4 Bring the cane over in a loop (about two fingers high) and pass it under the edge to the inside (fig. 74).

5 Pull the loop towards you so that it is upright and wind the end over the loop twice, spacing the twists evenly.

6 At the end of the second wrap, take the cane under the loop to the inside and thread it back under the ring to the inside.

7 Following the wraps, wind twice over the loop and then through to the outside.

8 Finish off the end by weaving it in and out with the other sticks below the handle (see fig. 73).

FINISHING OFF

Cut the ends of each of the sticks forming the main body of the tray. Use side cutters to make decorative diagonal cuts. The ends should rest on the edge of the tray without overlapping it (see the colour photograph).

PROJECT 8

Decorative spiral tray

In order to achieve this spiral weave with three-rod waling the number of base sticks must be divisible by the number of weavers plus two. I used 16 base sticks, which, when crossed at the centre, makes 32 sticks.

MATERIALS

For a tray with a diameter of 50cm (20in):

- No. 12 cane for base sticks
- Nos. 3 and 6 cane for weaving the base
- No. 15 cane for bye-stakes
- No. 6 cane for the side stakes
- No. 8 cane for upsetting the sides

Weight of tray 500g (1lb 2oz)

METHOD

The instructions for this tray have been kept to the bare minimum. Please refer back for detailed instructions, given on the pages referred to below.

1 From no. 12 cane cut 16 base sticks at least 10cm (4in) longer than the required diameter of the tray. As the base sticks of this decorative slath are pierced off centre, extra length may be required for adjustment after the 16 sticks are pushed together to form the slath.

2 Refer to the instructions for the Madeira Platter on how to construct the slath (see page 44).

3 Using no. 3 cane, pair round the slath three times and then open out the sticks into doubles. Pair round once or twice and open out into single sticks. Pair round twice more, until the sticks are opened out evenly. Compress the rows by pushing down firmly with the tip of a bodkin.

WALING

Using no. 3 cane work six rows of a three-rod wale. There is no need to change the stroke – as the whole tray is worked in waling, there is no 'spiralling up onto the next row', which is only noticeable when a band of a few rows of waling is woven.

Joining

Unlike normal joins in waling, all finishing and starting ends should be left at the back of the tray, each one resting behind a base stick. This is not as strong as the usual waling join (see page 18), but avoids interruption of the pattern.

WEAVING THE SPIRALS AND REVERSED SPIRALS

Follow the instructions for weaving three-rod spiral waling as given for the Cheese Tray (see page 41).

It is easiest to weave this tray on a flat surface, tightly pressing down each row with your fingers.

1 Using no. 6 cane work a three-rod wale. (I used two natural canes and one cane dyed with Tudor Black Oak wood dye). After four rows alter the thickness of the spirals by changing the second light-coloured cane for a dark one.

2 Weave another three rows and change so that all three are dark.

3 Weave four more rows to give a band of dark weaving. There are now eleven rows of waling.

4 Cut off all three canes and work six rows of waling **anti-clockwise**. I used brown, black and natural cane.

5 Next cut off the three ends, and with three new weavers (two brown and one natural) recommence waling in a **clockwise** direction.

Strengthening the base with bye-stakes

A tray needs to be firm and rigid, so cut one bye-stake for every stake from no. 15 cane. (No. 14 will do, or even white willow if not more than 0.5cm ($\frac{1}{4}$in) in diameter.)

Slype the ends and push one bye-stake down on the right-hand side of every stake as far as possible towards the centre.

6 After a few more rows change one of the brown canes to another natural, and a few rows further, the brown to a darkish red. The red finally becomes a solid colour by substituting for one then both of the two natural weavers.

STAKING UP AND WALING

1 From no. 6 cane cut two stakes for every bottom stick, 45cm (18in) long.

Slype the ends and soak them in warm water for five minutes.

2 Insert the 64 stakes, one on either side of each bottom stick together with its bye-stake.

3 Make a ring of no. 12 cane, twisting it round itself to make a circle slightly smaller than the tray (see figs. 71 and 72).

4 Squeeze all the stakes with round-nosed pliers close to the edge of the tray. Bend them up and put the ring around them to hold them up straight. Fix the ring in position by threading some of the stakes through the twists in the ring.

5 Using four lengths of damp no. 8 cane, work one round of a four-rod pull-down wale (see pages 31–33).

6 Drop one rod and continue with a three-rod wale. Work tightly for the next four rows, so the tray has a strong, straight edge. The fifth row need not be so tight.

PLAIT BORDER

Follow the instructions given for the plait border on pages 77–80. Because of the size of the tray, you may find it difficult to keep all the stakes in a damp, pliable condition. Carefully turn the stakes in a large sink of water (try not to get the coloured canes on the base wet), test for readiness (see page 22) and use a spray with warm water while you work. Avoid working in a heated room.

PROJECT 9

Cane ball

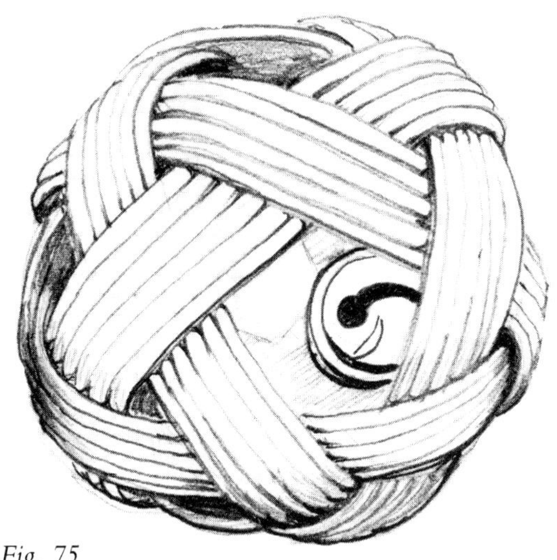

Fig. 75

Years ago I bought a cane ball like this one. It was sold as a rattle and had a bell suspended inside. I looked at it from all angles, asked lots of friends how they thought it had been made, all to no avail.

Later I found out that it was a copy of a ball used in south-east Asia for a game called Sepak Raga ('sepak' meaning kick and 'raga' woven ball). We had some Malaysian students living with us at that time but they couldn't think how it was made either. Finally, with the help of some friends in the Basketmakers' Association, I found out how it was constructed. After several attempts and some rather elliptical balls, I think this may be a foolproof method.

MATERIALS

For a ball with a circumference of 25cm (10in) and diameter of 8cm (3in):

- Six lengths of no. 3, 4 or 5 cane approximately 2m (79in) long
- Six short lengths of plastic packing tape in six different colours if possible (leftovers from parcels)
- Acrylic paints (optional)
- Sellotape
- Paperclips
- One bell of the sort used for toys, with a **secure** ring fastening

Weight 30g (1oz)

METHOD

1 Cut six lengths of packing tape, exactly 30cm (12in) long – I used five white and one blue, painting the white different colours with acrylic paints. Using a black marking pen draw a line across each tape 3cm ($1\frac{1}{4}$in) from each end. This marks where the overlap will be.

2 Number each piece at both ends, 1 and 1, 2 and 2, etc.

3 Place the first three pieces as shown in colour photo 1. The plastic packing tape usually has a bend to it – lay it concave side upwards. Fix with paperclips.

4 Now add pieces 4 and 5. Push them tightly together, making sure all the angles are the same. Fix with five paper clips (colour photo 2). For more stability sellotape strand no. 1 to a wooden board or plastic worktop while all the ends are joined together.

5 Make strand no. 6 (white with black line) into a circle and fix with sellotape, overlapping only 3cm ($1\frac{1}{4}$in) marked. Slip it into position as shown (colour photo 3).

6 Join the ends of strand no. 1 (purple), with sellotape carefully on the line.

Note Keep strand no. 1 straight across in front of you all the time you are working, otherwise you may get muddled.

Joining

Working in a clockwise direction from the top left towards you join 2, then 3, then 4 and finally 5.

7 Join the ends of 2 (yellow) over the top of 1 (colour photo 4).

8 Join the ends of 3 (red) under 1 and over 2.

9 Join the ends of 4 (blue) over 3 and 2, then towards you under 1.

10 Join the ends of 5 (green) over 1, under 3, over 4 and under 2 (colour photo 5).

This completes the pattern. There should be a pentagon at the top mirroring the one that was formed in the middle of the five-pointed star at the beginning. Every piece of tape should alternate over and under every other one that it passes. If it doesn't, remove all the sellotape with a sharp craft knife and start again. The more often you try the easier it becomes, and I speak from experience!

WEAVING IN THE CANE

1 When you finally have a round ball that you are satisfied with, take the first of the six lengths of cane (which has been soaked in warm water for about five minutes) and following no. 6, wind a complete circle round the ball, lying the cane on top of the tape and keeping it the same size.

2 Do the same with the next five lengths of cane, each in turn following the numbered tapes.

3 When each has made one complete circle of the ball, repeat the procedure with each in turn until all have circled the ball **twice**, keeping the working end to the left of each circle.

Note Keep dipping the canes in warm water while you work. It is very annoying

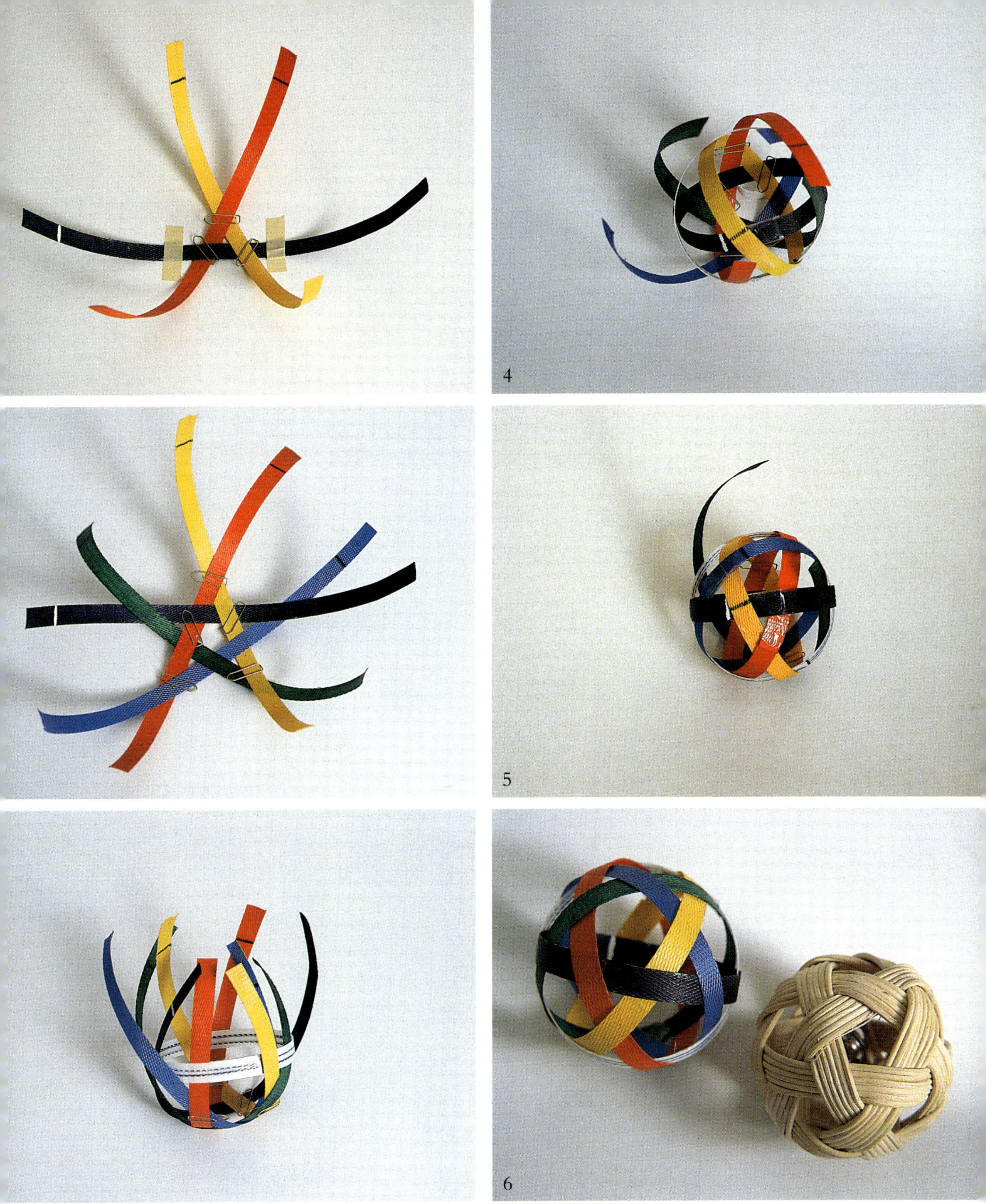

Making the Cane ball, step by step

(Above) *Fruit basket with scalloped border*

(Right) *Self-locking tray*

(Top right) *Madeira platter*

(Bottom right) *Cane and willow bread basket*

(Above) *Willow flower basket*

(Top right) *Doll's Moses basket*

(Bottom right) *Baby's Moses basket*

(Above) *Picnic basket with plaited montbretia leaves*

(Right) *Cheese tray*

(Far right) *Ali Baba basket*

Rag basket

Willow shopper

if one length cracks right at the end, as you cannot hide a join.

By keeping the working end of the cane to the left of each circle (see above), you will be threading down through the triangles and up through the pentagons. This makes working easier as the spaces fill up.

4 Adjust all the coils so they are exactly the same size and then carefully remove the tapes by cutting the sellotape with a sharp craft knife.

5 Weave each strand in turn a third time, making sure that each coil lies beside the next and that they do not cross each other.

6 Continue weaving each cane in turn until all the canes are woven five or six times round the ball. For a final adjustment, immerse the ball in warm water and push into shape.

7 Cut off the ends and hide them under the weaving.

Note Any paint which may have marked the cane can be washed off in water. Singe to remove any loose hairs (p. 9).

ADDING A BELL

To make a rattle thread a bell onto one of the canes while weaving the **third** circle, so that it is **securely fixed** in the **middle of a band of weaving** and will **not** come adrift.

VARIATIONS

(For the experienced weaver of cane balls!) Try making larger circles with different sizes of cane and in different colours. Make a lampshade. Or make a cane ball round the oasis used by dried flower arrangers; push lavender or other dried flowers or herbs through the pentagons and hang up the ball. There are endless possibilities.

PROJECT 10

Willow shopper or flower basket

This attractive basket is made with different-coloured willows. It could also be made with hedgerow material (see page 102) or commercially grown willow. All the techniques used to make this basket have already been explained. The only major difference is in the material; unlike manufactured cane which comes in continuous lengths of even thickness, each individual willow rod is thicker at one end than the other. This has to be compensated for in the weaving.

MATERIALS

For a basket with a side height of 16cm ($6\frac{1}{2}$in), base diameter 18cm (7in), border diameter 28cm (11in) and handle height from base 28cm (11in):

- One rod for the handle, about 2cm ($\frac{3}{4}$in) in diameter at the butt end
- Six rods about 5mm ($\frac{1}{4}$in) in diameter at the butt end for the base sticks
- 24 rods about 5mm ($\frac{1}{4}$in) in diameter at the butt end for the side stakes
- About 15–20 thin rods for pairing the base
- About 40–50 rods for waling the side (and wrapping the handle)

PREPARING THE MATERIALS

1 'Hedgerow materials' should be used within two to four weeks of cutting (see page 102), so they don't need soaking. However, they need to be kept outside in a damp place until they are used. If the basket is not made all in one go, its framework and the materials sorted for use all need to be kept in a cool, damp place – under a hedge for instance.

2 Commercially grown willow, buff or white, needs to be soaked for about half to one hour in cold water and then wrapped in a damp cloth (not wringing wet).

Allow the willow to mellow in a cool place (e.g. a garage) for four to six hours, or overnight, so that it becomes pliable.

Note Buff and white rods which have been stripped of their bark can only be kept damp for one or two days. After this they must be dried, otherwise mould will develop. They can be resoaked and used again another time.

3 'Brown willow' (this refers to any willow for basketmaking which has not been stripped) will need soaking for about two to three days in cold water, then wrapped overnight before use. It can be kept damp for up to a week in cool conditions.

Note These soaking times are for 1m (3ft) lengths of willow only. Larger rods need longer to soak.

Pitfall Never leave damp rods in plastic as they will quickly go mouldy.

The material I used was willow, of several different colours, which I had grown especially for basketmaking. It was harvested in January when the leaves were off and the sap was down, and then bundled up and put under a hedge to become 'clung' – this means partially dried but still pliable enough to weave. It could have been left to dry completely and then resoaked when needed.

METHOD

1 Cut six butt ends 24cm ($9\frac{1}{2}$in) long from the thicker rods.

2 Placing butts and tips alternately, make the slath – three rods through three as on pages 26 and 27 (see also fig. 76).

Note Most rods have a natural curve. Consider this and make use of it when making the slath, it will help to form the crown (see pages 29–30).

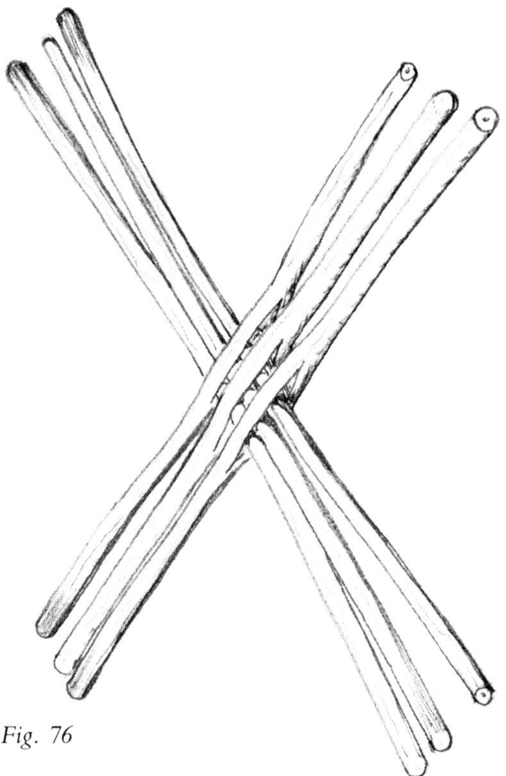

Fig. 76

3 Select two fine rods both the same length, and slip the tips into one of the slots in the slath. (Say that fast!) (see fig. 77)

4 Pair twice round to tie in the slath. After two rounds start to open out the bottom sticks (see page 29).

5 Continue pairing and opening out the sticks and gently forming the crown.

Joining

When one butt end is reached, join both butts next to each other. Make the join with the butts of another two matching rods (see figs. 30–31).

When the tips run out the join is made with tips, overlap the old and new tips for a few strokes.

6 When the base measures about 18cm

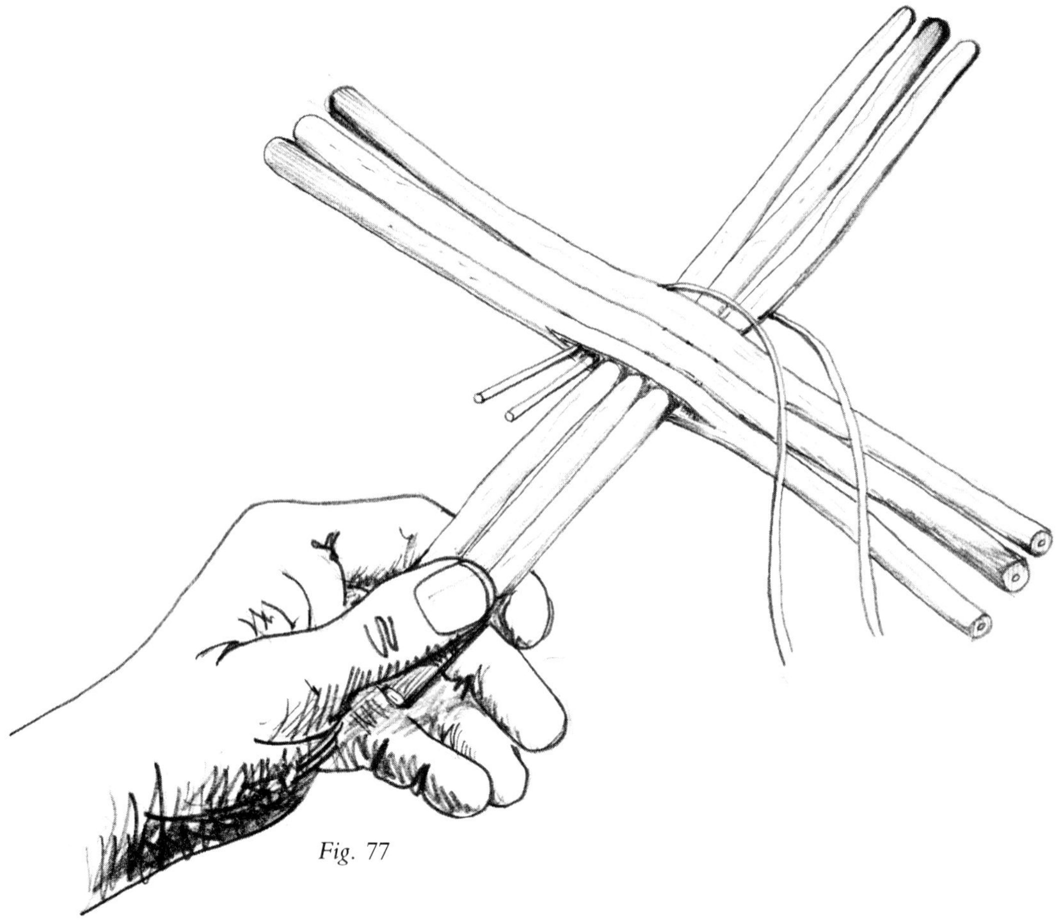

Fig. 77

(7in) finish with tips. (It would be difficult to make a smooth finish with butts.)

Note If you haven't enough time to finish the basket straight off, keep the materials somewhere where they will remain clung until you are ready to start again (hopefully, within a day or two). If you are using buff or white stripped willow it will need to dry out and be resoaked.

STAKING UP

In willow and hedgerow basketmaking, the side stakes are not cut to the required size as in canework. The whole willow rod is used and the excess cut off after the border is finished.

1 Making sure that the rods are in workable condition (pliable enough to bend round your fist without cracking), select 24 medium-sized rods for the side stakes – they should be stouter than the ones used for weaving the side, but not more than 0.5cm ($\frac{1}{4}$in) thick at the border. This means that if the stakes are pushed into the base 6cm ($2\frac{1}{2}$in) and the side of the basket measures 16cm ($6\frac{1}{2}$in), the border will be about 22cm (9in) up from the butt. Roughly check the thickness at this height, and if the rods are too thick cut some off the butt ends. The

Fig. 78

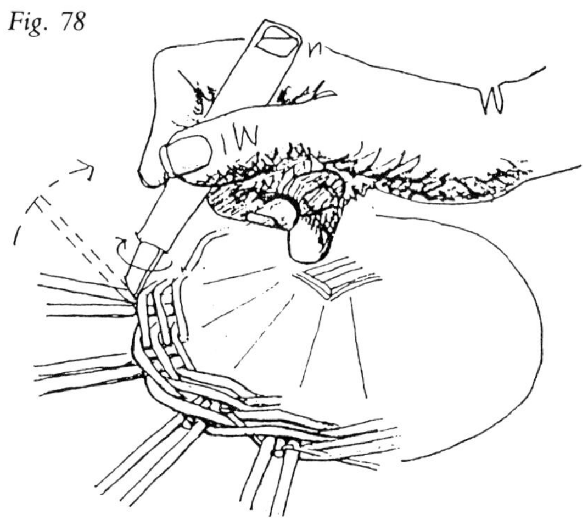

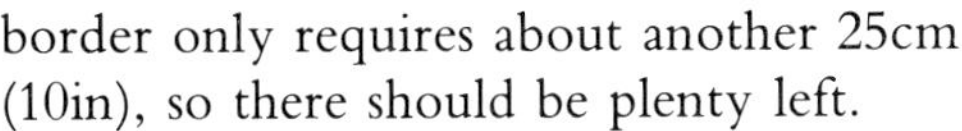

border only requires about another 25cm (10in), so there should be plenty left.

2 Slype the butt ends of the 24 rods, turn the base upside down (saucer right way up) and insert the rods well into the base, one at either side of each base stick. (Trim each base stick as you stake up.)

3 Turn the base over and trim off any ends on the convex side of the base. As this will be the inside it will be difficult to trim it later when the basket is finished.

PRICKING UP THE STAKES

1 With a sharp knife and the base on a firm surface (the floor is best), insert the tip of the knife into a side stake close to the edge of the base. The knife should **only** penetrate as far as the pith in the middle of the rod (fig. 78).

2 Lift the side stake and at the same time twist the knife a quarter turn. This enables the rod to be bent at a right angle without cracking.

3 Work round the base pricking up each stake in turn.

4 When all the stakes are pricked up tie them firmly with string.

Fig. 79

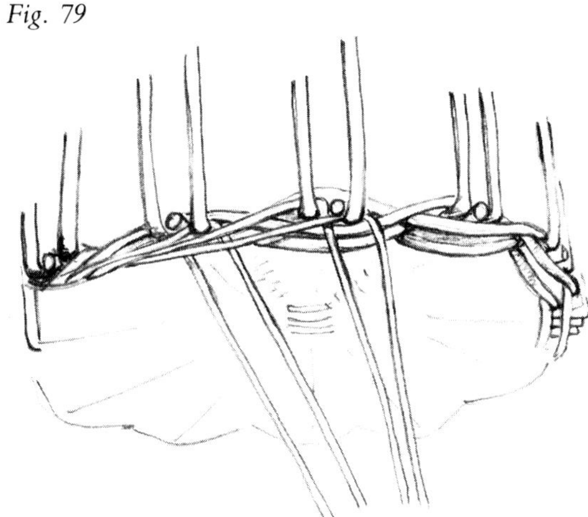

THE UPSETT

1 Making sure the rods are pliable and in good condition for working (see 'Preparing the materials' above). Select four rods of about equal length and thickness – they must be long enough to weave once round the base with a bit over.

2 With the basket on its side, work a four-rod pull-down wale (see page 31), starting by laying in the tips in four consecutive spaces (fig. 79).

3 At the end of the first round drop the first rod to reach the start and continue with the other three rods (fig. 80).

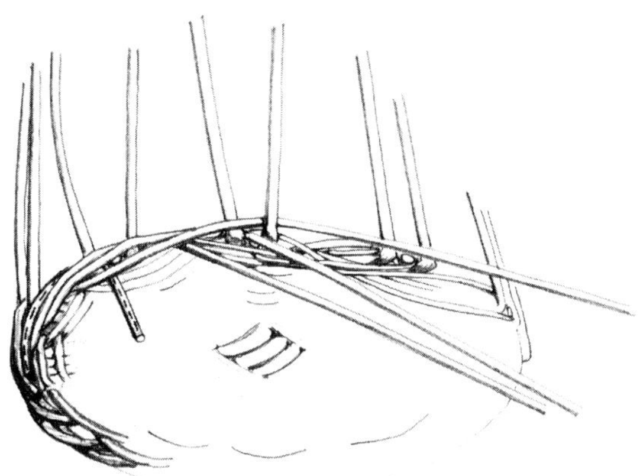

Fig. 80

The next three strokes (one for each rod) are taken in front of three and behind one, as in a four-rod wale. After this the weave continues as for a three-rod wale, in front of two and behind one.

4 Cut off the end of the dropped rod and trim off any other ends on the base. Stand the basket on a flat surface, put a weight inside and continue with a three-rod wale.

Note There is no need to change the stroke with willow or hedgerow material as the nature of the material is so irregular that no difference is noticed at the end of one row of waling and the beginning of the next.

Joining

When one of the three butts runs out, all three are joined at once with the butt end of new rods. Select three matching rods, join these next to each other, starting with the left-hand rod and weaving this before joining in the second and finally the third (see fig. 14).

5 Continue with the upsetting, shaping the basket by making the side stakes ease gently outwards a little. When the tip ends of the three rods are reached, remove the string. The stakes should by now be firmly positioned. If not, weave another round of waling using six rods, starting and finishing with tips.

Rap down the waling firmly.

WEAVING THE SIDE (FOUR-ROD WALE)

The whole of the side of this basket is woven in a four-rod wale. This weave gives a lovely dense, tightly woven basket and is especially suitable for hedgerow materials which vary in thickness, length and pliability.

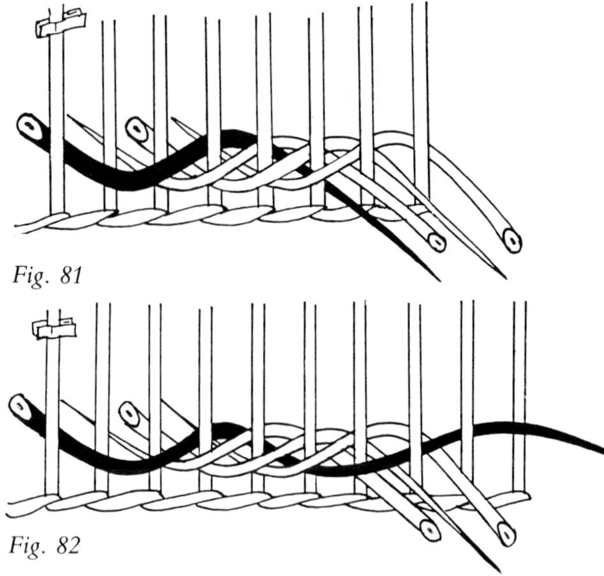

Fig. 81

Fig. 82

Note There is no need to use handle liners.

1 Mark a stake with a clothes peg or twist-tie.

2 Pick four rods (this time they need not match – any colour, any length). Place them in four consecutive spaces to the right of the marked stake, alternating butts and tips (fig. 81).

3 Work a wale with these four rods, always picking up the left-hand rod. Weave in front of **two** stakes and behind **two** each time (fig. 82).

4 Work twice round the basket, and when you pass the marked stake for the second time, compress the rows of weaving one upon the other by rapping them down with a rapping iron. (A small hammer will do, or a tyre lever or heavy file wrapped in a cloth so the bark is not damaged.)

Joining

Unlike the three- and four-rod wale used for upsetting, these rods are **not** joined all at the same time, but as they run out. Join when the short rod is in the left-hand position. Butts join to butts and tips to tips. Make sure you tuck the new end in to the right of the old one, not on top.

Note Be careful not to 'lose' one rod. Keep joining as necessary and continue to weave with four rods, rapping the weaving down after every two rows.

5 When the height of the basket measures about 15cm (6in) rap down the last row. Measuring the height of the basket from the table top all the way round, rap down any bits that are too high.

THREE-ROD PLAIN BORDER

If the rods have become dry they must be resoaked before the border is attempted – it won't hurt the whole basket to be immersed.

1 Bend all the stakes over gently to the right, being careful not to crack them. I find that bending the stakes over half a clothes peg on its side gives just the right height for the bend (fig. 83).

2 Work a three-rod border following the instructions on pages 50–54.

HANDLE

1 Slype the butt end of the rod you selected for the handle and push it down as far as possible into the side of the basket to the left of one of the side stakes. (You may need to open a space with a bodkin first.)

2 Gently coax the rod into the shape you want, cut it to the right length (the butt end could probably be inserted right down to the base). Slype and insert the tip end on the opposite side of the basket.

3 Select three or four long, slender rods and slype the butts. Push two into the waling on the left of one end of the handle to a depth of about 5cm (2in).

4 Wrap them carefully round the handle, making a wide curve in order to avoid kinks – they should wrap round about four times (see the colour photograph). Leave the ends inside.

5 Do exactly the same with the other rods, starting at the opposite end of the handle. (You can use just one rod this time if desired.) These rods should lie alongside the first when they are twisted round the handle. Leave the ends inside.

Note The handle bow is not completely covered by the rods.

FINISHING THE HANDLE

1 Making a gap in the siding under about two rows of waling, thread the tips of the wrapping rods through to the outside of the basket, up across the front, round the back of the handle on the left of the bow and across the front again to the right.

2 Thread back to the inside and weave the tips in and out of the weaving until they feel secure.

3 Do the same with the tips at the other end of the handle.

Note If the tips are too short for finishing as described, weave the ends in and out of the siding and wrap a pliable length of willow round each end of the handle (see

Fig. 83

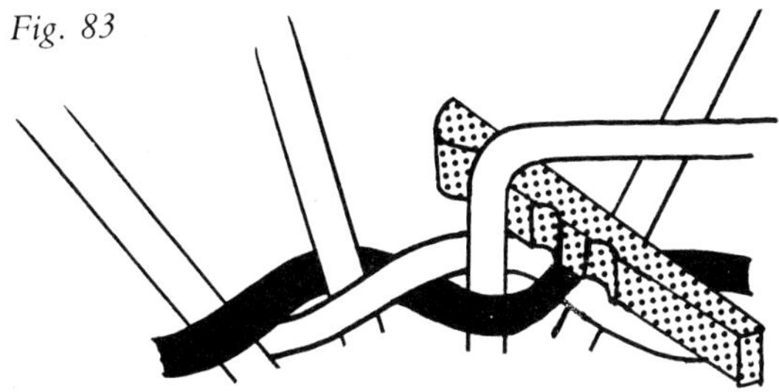

colour photo of the cane and Willow Bread Basket). Catch the butt end of the length of willow in under these wraps and weave its tip, or finishing end, into the siding.

PEGGING THE HANDLE

In order to prevent the handle from pulling out, insert a peg through the waling and handle bow.

1 Drive a bodkin through at an oblique angle, so that the peg will blend in with the waling.

2 Cut a piece of dry willow (wet would bend) about 5cm (2in) long. Withdraw the bodkin and hammer the peg through in its place.

3 Repeat at the other side and trim any protruding ends (see fig. 49).

PICKING OFF THE BASKET

'Picking off' is the last job in making the basket and means cutting off the spare ends. You may like to leave some of the tip ends on the outside if you are going to use the basket for flower arranging (see the photo). However, if the basket is to be used for shopping, these ends might prove a hazard!

PROJECT 11

Doll's Moses basket

If you want to make this doll's basket with the sides woven in a rush plait you will need about 12 to 14 metres (13 to 15 yards) of 1cm ($\frac{1}{2}$in) wide plait. Other materials could be used just as well (see Rag Basket, p. 11). The basket illustrated here was made especially for the Inuit doll.

If you want to make a basket of a different size to fit a special doll or teddy bear, instructions for designing your own oval basket are given at the end of this chapter.

MATERIALS

For a basket with a base 33cm × 15cm (13in × 6in), height 13cm (5in) at the foot end and 18cm (7in) at the head, and border measurement 42cm × 23cm (16$\frac{1}{2}$in × 9in):

- No. 3 cane for chain pairing the base
- No. 6 cane for the upsett and bye-stakes
- No. 8 cane for the stakes and top waling
- No. 12 or 14 cane for the base sticks
- Chair cane for wrapping the slath
- 12–14m (13–15 yards) of rush plait 1cm ($\frac{1}{2}$in) wide (for details of preparation, see end of chapter)

METHOD

From no. 12 or 14 cane cut three long base sticks 36cm (14in) and 11 short sticks 20cm (8in) long. These are a little longer than needed for the finished size to allow ease of working.

FORMING THE SLATH

1 Make a split in the centre of each short stick with the point of a craft knife and thread them all onto a bodkin.

2 Slype one end of each of the long sticks, thread one through on each side the bodkin. Remove the bodkin and thread through the third long stick in its place.

3 Soak for five minutes.

4 Check that all the sticks are positioned correctly (see fig. 84). There should be approximately 2cm ($\frac{3}{4}$in) between the middle of each short stick and the middle of the next.

5 Wrap the slath with chair cane as shown (figs. 103–104). This is not absolutely necessary but helps to keep the short sticks evenly spaced. A very small size of cane can be used if no chair cane is available–

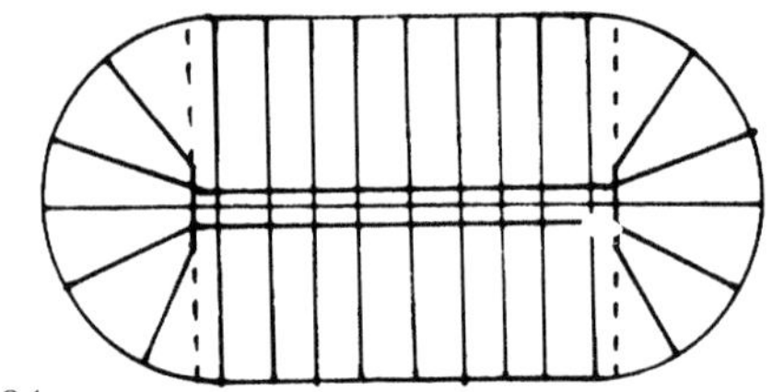

Fig. 84

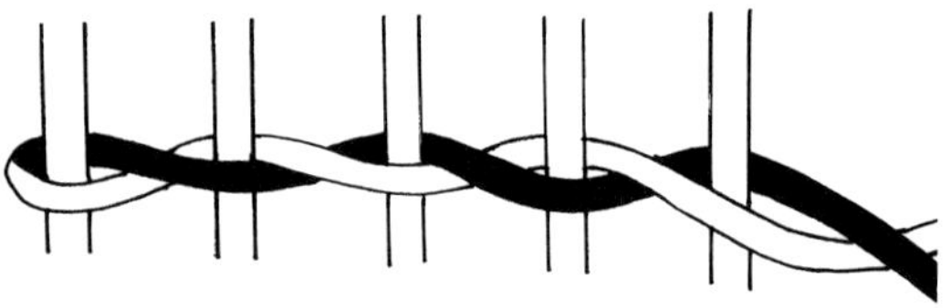

Fig. 85

bleached cane or string are the most pliable. Do not wrap too tightly or the long sticks may overlap.

CHAIN-PAIRING

'Chain-pairing' is weaving with one row of pairing (see fig. 25), followed by one row of reverse pairing (fig. 85), the two rows together forming a chain. It is a decorative weave and prevents the twist which occurs if a base is paired throughout. By pairing one row and then reversing the next the twist is counteracted. Randing a base also prevents a twist (see pages 85–87).

1 Slip a dry piece of no. 6 cane into the splits on each side of the wrapped slath (see fig. 103). These will help stop the weaving from becoming 'waisted' at the sides (dog bone effect).

2 Damp two long pieces of no. 3 cane. Bend them sharply (see Note, p. 28) near the middle (but not in the middle, otherwise both ends will run out at the same time).

3 Hook one loop round the long sticks at one end of the slath and weave a row of pairing along one side. When the other end of the long sticks is reached, hook the other length round them and weave reverse pairing (fig. 86).

Continue reverse pairing, right round the slath, overlapping the **first row** of pairing but **not** overtaking the ends.

4 Pick up the first weavers and pair right round the slath.

5 Now you have tied the slath with two rounds. Open out the sticks as shown in fig. 88 and continue chasing (see fig. 36) with pairing and reverse pairing. Weave one row of each alternately.

Note The cane used for pairing at the beginning will be used for pairing throughout the base and the other cane for the reverse pairing. Mark the ends of the canes used for reverse pairing to prevent confusion.

Joining

Joining should be done on the straight sides. Stagger the joins.

The reverse pairing join is exactly like the pairing join, only it is done from the **back** (see fig. 87).

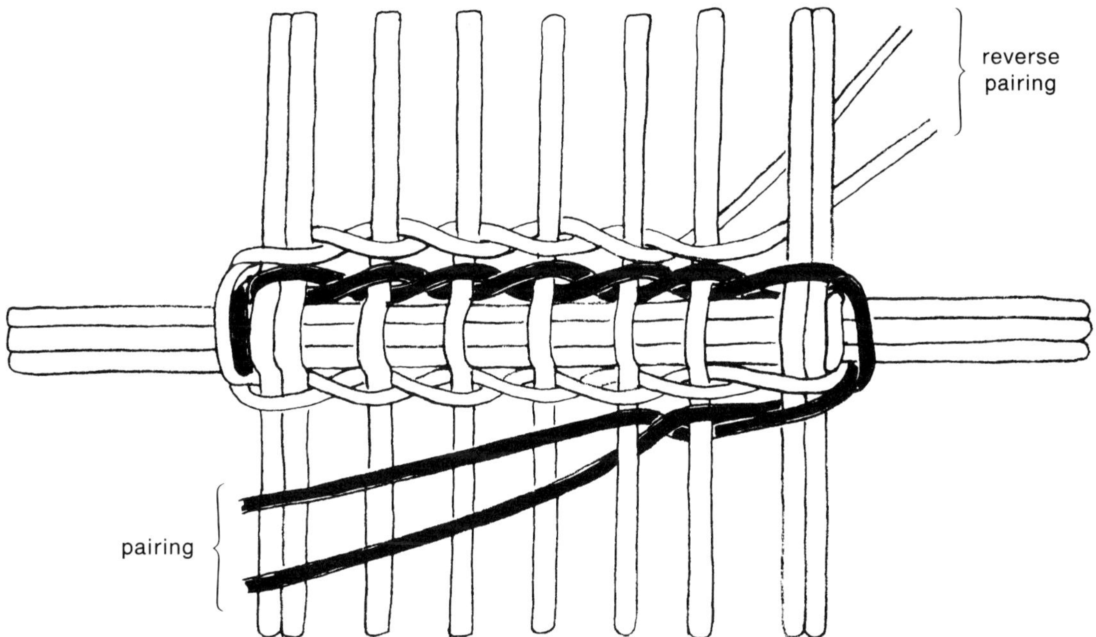

Fig. 86

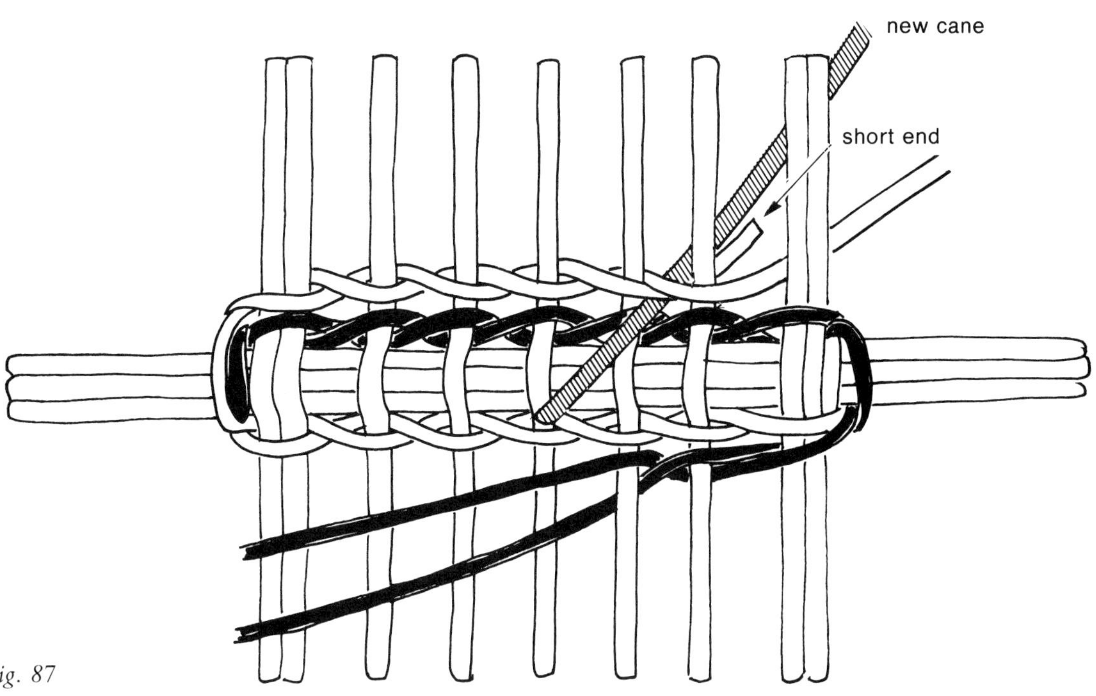

Fig. 87

Note If the base does start to twist slightly, bend it the opposite way while working.

6 After five rows of the chain start to crown the base (see page 29).

7 Continue chain-pairing until just one more row needs to be woven to bring the base to the required size. Secure the unwoven ends with a clothes peg. Do not cut them off.

STAKING UP

1 From no. 8 cane cut 14 side stakes 58cm (23in) and 24 stakes 50cm ($19\frac{1}{2}$in) long. The 14 longer ones are to be placed at the head end.

2 Slype one end of each stake and push well down into the base – one beside each stick along the straight sides and one on either side of each stick at the curved ends (see fig. 88).

Note Make sure that the 14 longer stakes are all positioned at one end.

3 **Before** bending the stakes up to form the side, weave the last round of pairing (or reverse pairing), opening out the pairs of stakes at each end with the weaving. Thread away the weavers and cut them off.

4 Soak the slath and stakes at the point where they are to be bent up. Squeeze the stakes with round-nosed pliers where they emerge from the base and gently bend

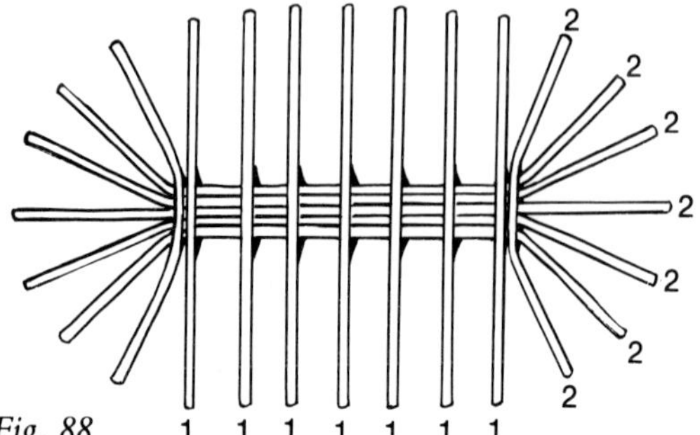

Fig. 88

upwards at a right angle. Tie up or fasten in three groups, one at each end and one in the middle, with elastic bands.

THE UPSETT

1 Starting on the long side, and with two full lengths of no. 6 cane, work a tight four-rod wale (see figs. 34–35) followed by three rows of three-rod wale.

2 Undo the elastic bands after two rows of three-rod if the stakes are well set up.

3 Remember to change the stroke correctly and avoid joining at this point. Finish correctly (see figs. 15–17).

BYE-STAKES

Using no. 8 cane, add one bye-stake on the right-hand side of each stake, making sure that those next to the longer stakes at the head end are at least 5cm (2in) longer than the others. They should all be cut to the required depth of the basket. (Mine were about 12cm (5in) and 17cm (7in).)

ADDING THE RUSH PLAIT

(For preparation, see pages 79–80)

1 Tuck the start of the plait behind a stake and bye-stake on the side of the basket (remember to put a weight inside to keep it steady), leaving an end to glue into place later. Weave the plait in and out all round the basket, taking care not to either push the stakes inwards or pull them out too much.

Note Because there is an even number of stakes, it is not possible to weave the whole side with the plait only, as it would travel in front and behind the same stakes each time. Therefore a chasing weave is used – one row of plait, one row of cane.

2 When the beginning is reached, start chasing with a length of no. 6 cane (fig. 36).

Fig. 89

3 Continue with one row plait, one row cane until the basket reaches the required height.

4 Start to 'build up' the head end with the plait only. Weave the plait round the head end to the last long stake on the other side. Wrap round that stake and weave back to the stake on the opposite side, round that and back again to one stake nearer the head. Continue building up, leaving out the last stake of each row, until the end is high enough (fig. 89). Then weave the plait once more right round the basket. This helps to hide the gap caused by turning round the stake when building up (sometimes known as 'packing').

5 Stop at the most appropriate place, leaving an end long enough to be glued later.

WALING

Work two rows of a three-rod wale (see pages 15–20) with no. 8 cane.

THREE-PAIR PLAIT

Now comes the tricky part! The border stakes have to be thoroughly damp and mellow so they won't crack when the border is woven, but the rush plait must not get wet.

1 Fill a large sink or bath with hot water and carefully turn the top of the basket in the water, wetting down to and including the waling. You could also carefully pour a kettle of hot water over the stakes at the point where they will be bent over. Test the end of one to see if it bends without cracking before starting the plait. Work in a cool place and keep the stakes damp with a spray if necessary.

2 Cut two pieces of no. 8 cane 10cm (4in) long and three pieces the length of the stakes above the wale plus about 5cm (2in).

Note It is very important that these pieces are the same thickness as the border stakes.

3 Squeeze all the stakes 0.5cm ($\frac{1}{4}$in) above the top of the wale with round-nosed pliers.

4 Place one of the short canes between two stakes (but not directly over the finish of the waling). Bend the stake to its left down over it and place one of the long pieces (known as 'feeders') beside it, leaving **at least** 5cm (2in) on the inside of the basket for finishing at the end (fig. 90).

5 Put in the second short piece, making

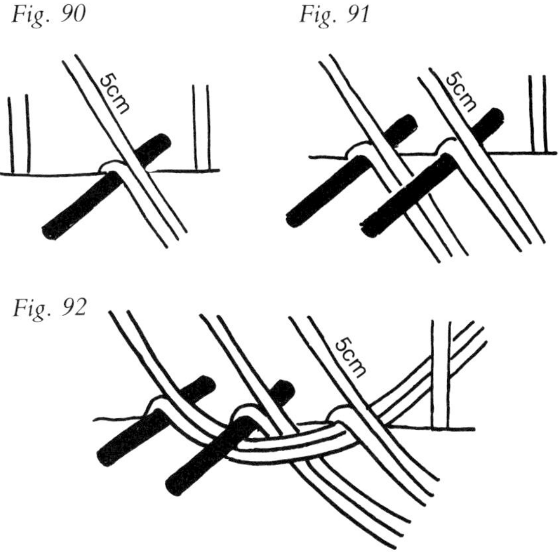

Fig. 90 *Fig. 91* *Fig. 92*

sure it overlaps the first two strands on the outside and place the second feeder beside it, leaving 5cm (2in) as before (fig. 91).

6 Pick up the first two canes on the outside (the pair on the left) and bring them through to the inside between the next two standing stakes. Bend down the left of these two stakes, and place the last feeder beside it.

Note Now all the extra pieces of cane are in place, each should have a 5cm (2in) end pointing to the left on the inside of the basket. There is now one pair on the inside and two pairs on the outside (fig. 92).

7 Pick up the left-hand pair on the outside ('pick up two') and take them between the next two stakes to the right ('take them through') (fig. 93).

8 Bend down the left-hand stake ('bend down the stake'). Bring out the left-hand pair beside it ('and bring out two'). This makes the first group of three on the outside (figs. 94–95).

Note You will find it easier to make a good plait if you have a weight inside the basket and stand directly over the border as you work.

9 Repeat this movement, picking up the left-hand pair on the outside:

Pick up two,
Take them through,
Bend down the stake
And bring out two.

Note There should now be three stakes in each of the two groups on the outside and one pair on the inside (fig. 96).

Each time you 'pick up two' it means A and B – C is left behind and trimmed off at the end. It is most important to take the correct two, A and B, **not** C (fig. 97).

You will find by working systematically that one hand is keeping the plait in place, leaving the other free to weave the border. They alternate with each stroke.

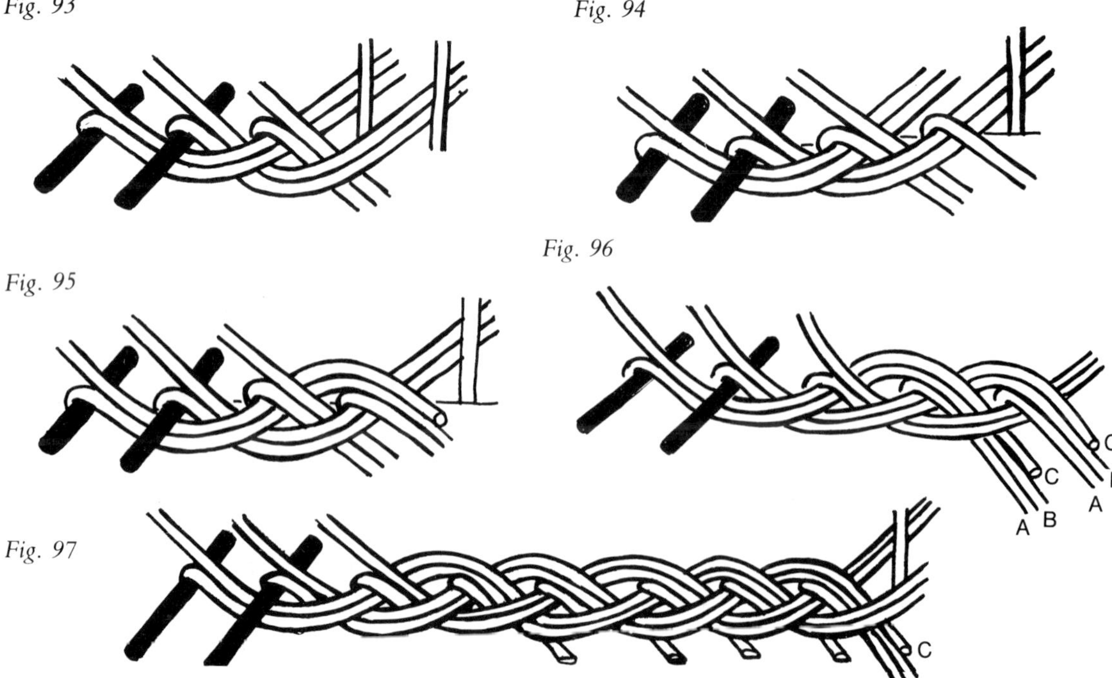

Fig. 93

Fig. 94

Fig. 95

Fig. 96

Fig. 97

Fig. 98

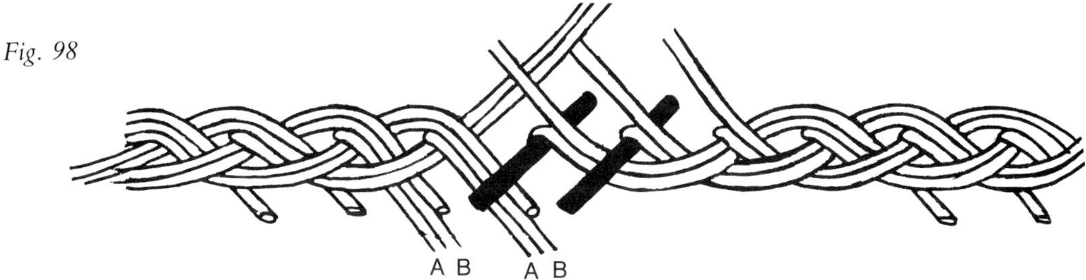

Fig. 99

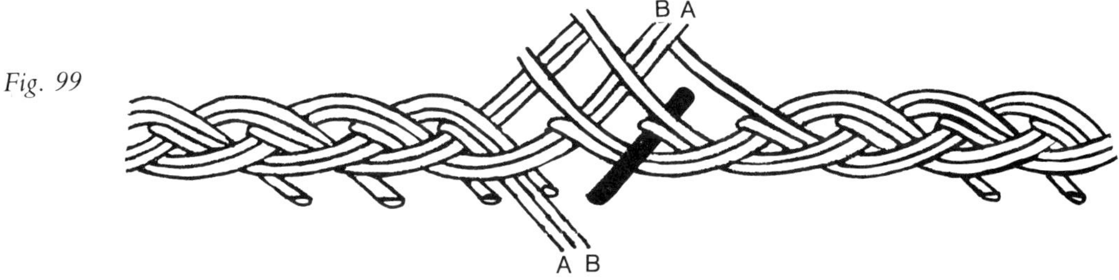

10 The plait continues with four distinct movements:

- *Pick up two* (lifting with the back of the left thumb while holding the other four stakes below)
- *Take them through* (with the right hand which then holds them in place)
- *Bend down the stake* (with the left thumb, easing it over firmly on top of the border).

Everything is now held secure by this last stroke, leaving the right hand free to

- *Bring out two*

11 Continue round the border until there are no stakes left standing upright (fig. 98).

FINISHING OFF

1 Pick up two (A and B) and take them through to the inside, following the **first** short stick, over the last three brought out. The first short stick can now be removed (fig. 99).

2 Pick up two again, the last A and B on the outside, and take them through, following **exactly** where the second short stick lies over the first pair. Now remove this short stick. The weave will look like fig. 100A.

3 There are now three single ends pointing left (shaded) and three pairs pointing right. Weave the single long ends away under the border and out to the front (see fig. 100B).

Weave the right-hand cane of each pair (spotted) into the border, following the pattern (see fig. 100C).

4 Cut off the three remaining ends on the inside. Turn the basket upside down and trim the ends underneath the plait. Using side cutters pick off any other protruding ends and, if necessary, glue the start and finish of the rush plait.

PREPARING THE RUSHES

(For plaiting instructions see page 92)

Rushes are harvested in summer (July/August), dried (which may take as long as four weeks) and then stored.

Fig. 100A

Fig. 100B

Fig. 100C

To prepare them for use, lay them on the ground and water them. Sprinkle a blanket with water, then put the wet rushes on the blanket and wrap up tightly for about three hours or overnight until they are soft and pliable. Do not prepare more than you have time to plait, as they cannot be kept damp for longer than 24 hours. Dry those not used.

DESIGNING AN OVAL BASKET

To make a Moses Basket to fit a special doll or teddy bear, first draw an oval round the toy leaving a 2.5cm (1in) margin.

Using a compass, draw a circle to fit into each end of the oval – the diameter of the circles should be the width of the oval. (The width of my basket was 14cm ($5\frac{1}{2}$in), so the diameter of the circles was also 14cm.)

The base will be made up of two semi-circles joined by straight lines of the required length. The overall length of my basket base was 33cm (13in). The length of the lines joining the two semi-circles is therefore 18cm (7in). Draw in the straight lines (fig. 101).

Fig. 101

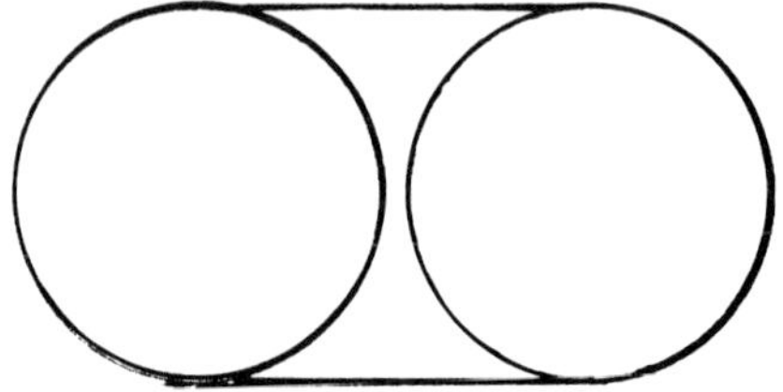

CALCULATING THE NUMBER OF BASE STICKS

An oval base is made up of three, four, five or six long sticks (horizontal) and a number of shorter sticks (vertical), depending on the size of the basket.

As you can see from the colour photo, the basket slopes outwards, so its top edge will have a larger circumference than its base.

Note When designing a basket, a professional basketmaker first calculates the widest part of the basket (usually the top edge). According to the thickness of the material to be used, the stakes at this place need to be close enough together to keep the shape rigid.

The more outward slope a basket has, the closer the stakes will have to be at the base.

In order to keep the instructions as uncomplicated as possible, we will work out the circumference of the **base** and, marking it on the paper pattern, place the stakes 2cm ($\frac{3}{4}$in) apart. This will allow enough outward flow for a small Moses Basket and the stakes at the border won't be more than 2.5cm to 4cm (1–1$\frac{1}{2}$in) apart.

In order to understand how the stakes will be placed in an oval, it is first necessary to understand the construction of a circular base.

1 First calculate the number of **bottom sticks**. To find out how the sticks will be placed you will have to work out the circumference of one of the circles and then understand how the base sticks fit into the circle.

2 In my basket the diameter of the circles was 14cm (5$\frac{1}{2}$in), the same width as the base.

3 To calculate roughly the circumference of a circle, multiply the diameter by three, and add on one-seventh.

4 The diameter was 14cm (5$\frac{1}{2}$in):

14cm × 3 = 42
14cm ÷ 7 = 2
42 + 2 = **44cm**

So if the circumference of the circle is 44cm, how many base sticks will be needed? Each base stick in a **circle** has two side stakes at **each** end, so each stick 'carries' four side stakes (see fig. 32).

5 The side stakes need to be about 2cm ($\frac{3}{4}$in) apart at the edge of the base, so that means approximately 22 stakes for the 44cm circumference. Twenty-two divided by four won't go exactly, so call it 24. Twenty-four side stakes require six bottom sticks. Eureka! (Now you know how to determine how many sticks and stakes are needed for a round basket!)

6 However, as you are considering an **oval**, only half a circle is used at each end (see fig. 88). So the circumference of the oval will be one complete circle measuring 44cm (17$\frac{1}{4}$in) plus two straight sides measuring 18cm (7in).

44 + 18 + 18 = **80cm**

7 The circumference of the base is about 80cm (31$\frac{1}{2}$in) so about 40 side stakes will be needed. (In fact, I used 38.)

8 The semi-circles are made up of the ends of the three long (horizontal) sticks and two short (vertical) sticks (see fig. 102). The sticks which fan out all carry two side stakes at each end and the others carry one at each end

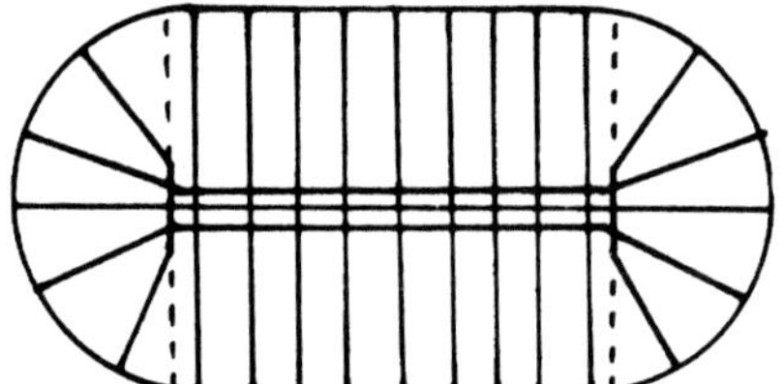

Fig. 102

(fig. 88). As there are twelve side stakes to each semi-circle, you will need three long base sticks. Mark them on your plan (fig. 102).

Note Fig. 105 shows a base with five long sticks. A wider base requires more long sticks and longer short sticks. The number is again determined by the circumference of the circles.

9 The short sticks along the sides carry only one side stake at each end so we need seven more to carry 38 side stakes or eight to carry 40. Spacing them evenly, mark these on the plan.

10 I used three long sticks and eleven short ones. The short ones were spaced exactly 2cm ($\frac{3}{4}$in) apart. Alternatively, I could have fitted in one more short stick and had 40 side stakes.

11 Allow 2cm (1in) extra at each end of the base sticks for ease of working. The three long sticks will be 38cm (15in) and the 11 short will be 20cm (8in).

CALCULATING THE LENGTH OF THE SIDE STAKES

Finally decide on the height of the basket. Sit the doll up and measure how much you want her to see! Will she fall out? For my basket 12cm (5in) seemed about right.
The length of the side stakes needed for the basket illustrated:

- 7cm (3in) to insert into the base
- plus 12cm (5in) for the side of the basket
- plus 30cm (12in) for the three-pair plait border
- adding about 8cm (3in) to the stakes at the head end to allow for the additional height.

PROJECT 12

Baby's Moses basket

The basket shown in the photograph was made in one of my classes by Sue Hunt for her son Jonathan. He used it night and day for about five months and it still looks as good as new!

MATERIALS

For an oval basket 80cm (31in) long, 38cm (15in) wide, 36cm (14in) high at the head end and 23cm (9in) high at the foot end:

- A homemade oval plywood base 80cm (31in) long by 38cm (15in) wide, with 77 holes drilled 2.5cm (1in) apart around the edge

Note There must be an **uneven** number of holes in the base in order to weave the plait continuously, otherwise a chasing weave will be necessary as in the Doll's Moses Basket.

- No. 8 cane for the stakes, bye-stakes and waling
- No. 10 cane for wrapping the handles
- 8mm ($\frac{5}{16}$in) cane for the handle bows

Rush plait

The measurement round the outside of the basket under the top waling is 230cm (90in). Multiply this by nine for the nine rows of plait and add some which will be taken up by the weaving (lots!). The measurement round the head end where the rush plait is 'built up' (see fig. 89) is 1m (40in). Multiply this by nine rows. This will give you some idea about how much material to plait, although you can always plait more as you weave the basket.

Pitfall Because of the shape of the basket, the stakes may be as much as 4cm ($1\frac{1}{2}$in) apart at the border, so you will need about 40cm (16in) of stake left to weave the three-pair plait border.

Do **not** allow the stakes to become further apart than 4cm ($1\frac{1}{2}$in) at the border, so be careful that the sides do not slope out too much.

METHOD

Work as for the Doll's Moses Basket, with the following differences.

1 The length of the stakes should be calculated by adding to the required height 7cm (3in) for the foot trac, plus at least 40cm (16in) for the three-pair plait. Do not forget to add extra length to the stakes at the head end. See the photograph to estimate how many longer stakes you will need.

2 Stake up and work a foot trac as for the Rag Basket.

3 Add handle liners (see p. 20) after the first few rows of waling and plait have been woven.

4 Use the colour photo as a guide when 'building up' the head end.

5 For the handles choose a piece of handle cane for the bow which is long enough for each end to reach down to the wooden base. Make a long gradual slype at each end to facilitate this and use a long bodkin to make a channel through the weaving, as this will help you to insert the handles.

Wrap the handles as for the Cane and Willow Bread Basket using no. 10 cane. **Be sure** to peg the handles.

PROJECT 13

Flower-gathering basket

I made this basket in April, using twigs from our garden dogwood together with seagrass to weave the side. The dogwood had been cut about three weeks before when pruning, and the material was stored under a hedge to dry out a little before use (but not so much that it cracked when worked). Any colourful and pliable twigs could have been used, but anything thicker than about 3mm ($\frac{1}{8}$in) at the thick end would have been too strong in relation to the side stakes of the basket.

The pieces I used were anything from 25–45cm (10–18ins) in length, and I needed about 50 of them.

Further information on the use of 'hedgerow' material can be found on page 102.

MATERIALS

For a basket with a base 30cm × 14cm (12in × 5$\frac{1}{2}$in), height 14cm (5$\frac{1}{2}$in) and top 50cm × 25cm (20in × 10in):

- No. 14 cane for the base sticks
- No. 6 or 8 cane (two short pieces) for the slath
- No. 8 cane for the side stakes and top waling
- No. 6 cane for the bye-stakes, upsett, weaving the base and **final** wrapping of the handles
- No. 3 cane for weaving the base and wrapping the handles
- Two pieces of handle cane
- Seagrass for weaving the side
- Twigs of dogwood to weave alternate rows with the seagrass and to decorate the handle

Weight of basket 500g (1lb 2oz)

METHOD

The ends of this basket slope (or flow) out more than in the baskets seen previously. To achieve this more long base sticks are needed.

1 Cut six base sticks 36cm (14in) and 11 sticks 20cm (8in).

2 Make a slath as for the Doll's Moses Basket. The pairs of end sticks will be 17cm (6$\frac{3}{4}$in) apart. Slip in the two short pieces of no. 6 or 8 cane as in fig. 103.

RANDING THE BASE

1 Take two lengths of damp no. 3 cane and slip the ends down the slots on opposite

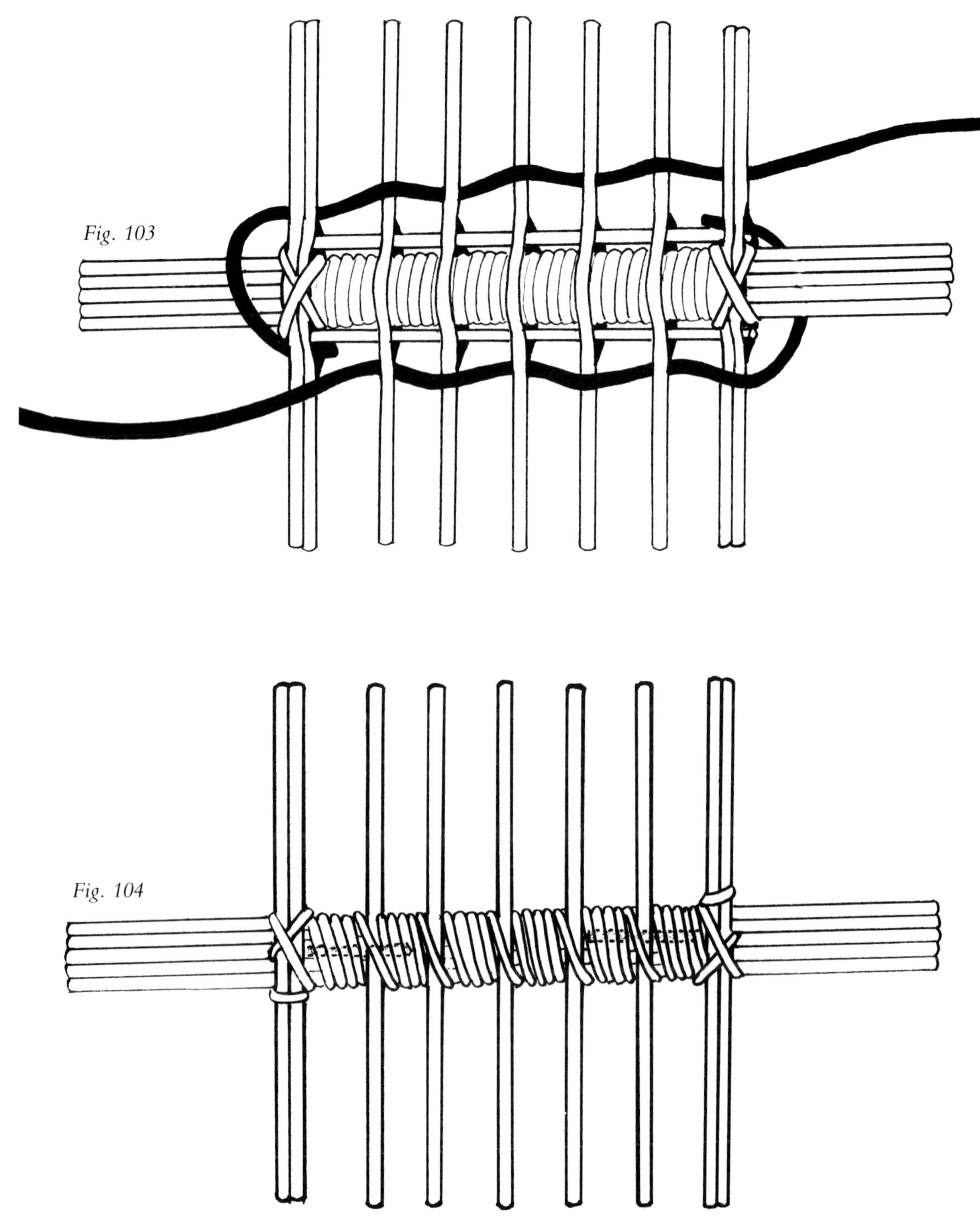

Fig. 103

Fig. 104

ends of the slath. These two canes will be chasing each other, going in front and behind alternate sticks. Therefore one starts by going in front of the group of long sticks at one end, and the other by going behind the group of long sticks at the other end (figs. 103–104).

2 Tie in the slath with two bands of randing round the groups of sticks.

3 Open out the end sticks into doubles and rand firmly round for another two rows, spacing the sticks evenly.

Note Use the tip of a bodkin to push down the rows of randing firmly between the sticks.

4 On the next row open all the sticks into singles. Working firmly and carefully, bring each of the strands of no. 3 cane first to the front of a bottom stick and then to the back. Adjust the sticks continually so the spaces become equal, bending them over slightly so the base becomes crowned (see p. 29) and compressing the rows down one upon the other so the base is strong and tight.

5 Work another ten rounds with no. 3 cane and then change to no. 6 to give the base more strength. Add another eight rows and finally weave a row of pairing to finish the edge firmly, tucking the ends into the row below.

STAKING UP

1 Cut 50 side stakes from no. 8 cane (natural) 50cm (20in) long. Slype the ends, soak for five minutes and stake up the base, one stake at each end of the short sticks, two at each end round the curve (figs. 88, 105).

2 Bend the stakes up as in fig. 33. Tie up the stakes in three lots with elastic bands or string.

THE UPSETT

Work a four-rod pull-down wale (see figs. 34–35).

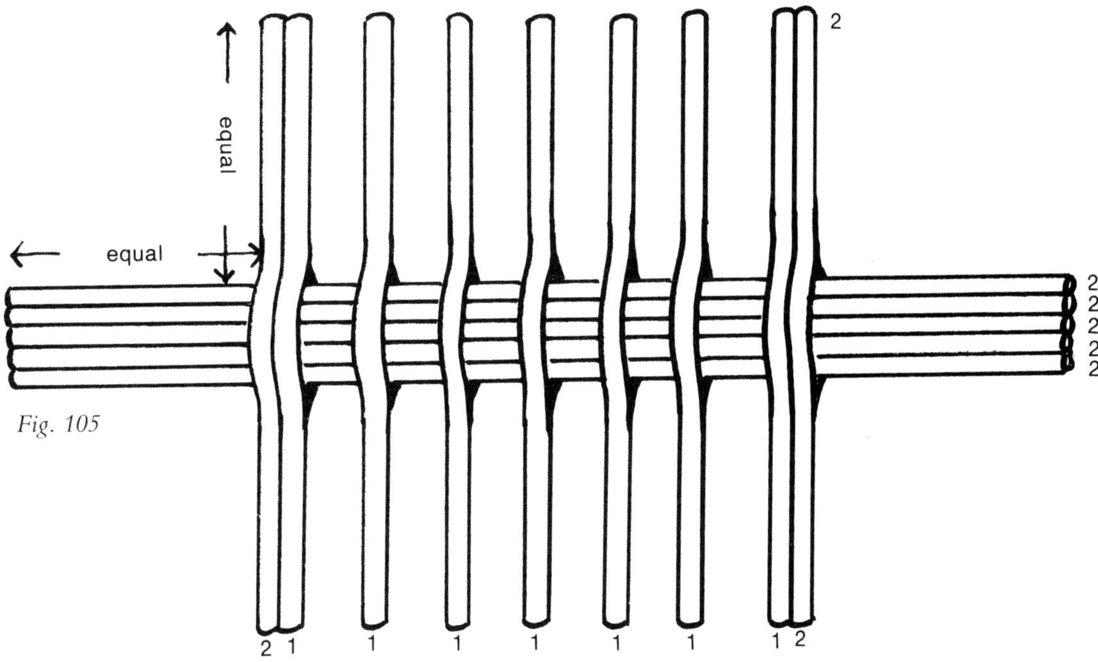

Fig. 105

1 Start on a long side of the basket and mark the stake to the left of the first of the four canes, so you will know where to change the stroke.

2 Work round the base with the four-rod wale until the marked stake is reached. Drop one cane and change the stroke (still in front of three and behind one). (See pages 31–33).

3 Cut the end of the dropped rod and weave it through to the inside.

SHAPING THE UPSETT

1 Stand the basket on a table with a weight inside and work a three-rod wale, upsetting the stakes so they flow slightly outwards.

2 Do not pull the weavers any more. Work with the index finger of your left hand behind the two stakes you are weaving across, pulling them outwards with every stroke until the rows of upsetting begin to hold the side stakes at the desired angle.

3 Change the stroke each time you reach the marked stake. Continually watch the shape: after three rows of the three-rod wale try undoing the elastic bands – if the stakes do not hold the shape replace the bands and continue with another round. After four rounds of three-rod waling the stakes should be firmly held. Finish the waling correctly (see pages 19–20).

4 Rap down the work firmly with a rapping iron to make sure it is even and there are no gaps between rows.

BYE-STAKES

Using no. 6 cane cut another 50 stakes 46cm (18in) long. Slype one end of each and, holding the basket on its side, push one bye-stake down through the waling on the right of each stake.

WEAVING THE SIDE (using seagrass and garden dogwood)

The side could be woven with natural cane, coloured cane, seagrass, rush, other hedgerow materials or almost anything weavable!

1 Begin with one row of seagrass, weaving it in and out of the stakes.

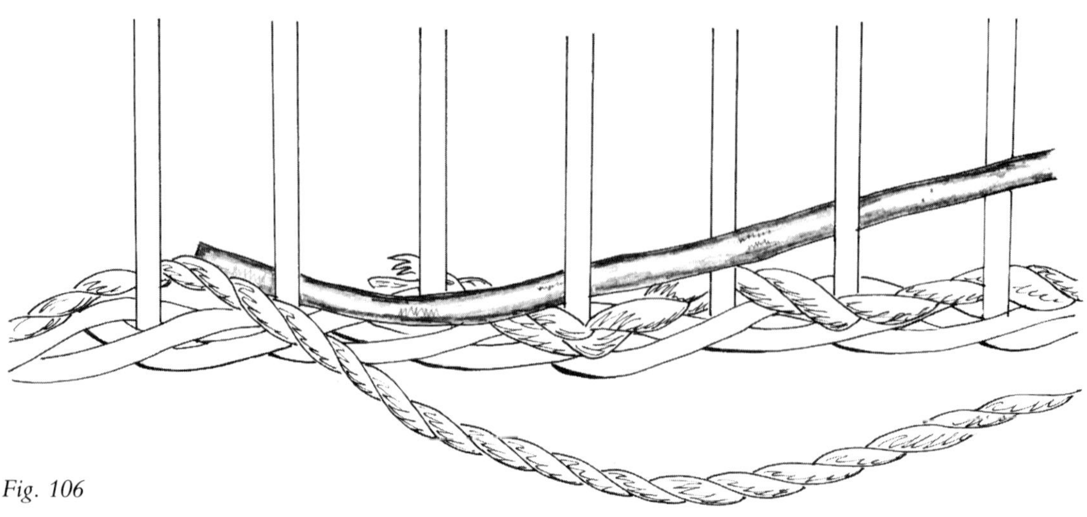

Fig. 106

2 When the start is reached drop the end of the seagrass, but do not cut it off.

3 Take the first piece of dogwood. Lay the butt end, which should be no thicker than the diameter of the no. 8 cane, on the inside of the basket, against the last stake that the seagrass reached (fig. 106).

Weave it in and out of the opposite side stakes to the row of seagrass. When you reach the tip end of the twig, leave it on the inside of the basket and join in another butt, joining as in randing (see fig. 39).

4 Carry on and complete the row, joining in new pieces as necessary until you reach the end of the strand of seagrass, which is then picked up and used to weave the next row.

5 Continue to weave in a row of seagrasss followed by a row of dogwood, carefully shaping the basket, watching to see that one end doesn't flow out further than the other and that the sides are kept fairly upright.

HANDLE LINERS

It is important to keep in mind the position of the handles. Put handle liners in place now (as for the Rag Basket), one stake out from the centre on each side, so you can see that they are going to be opposite each other. If they are not, adjustments will need to be made during the weaving, so they are not off balance.

6 After seven rows of dogwood and eight rows of seagrass change the positions of the two materials, either by cutting off the seagrass, or by taking it across behind two stakes instead of one at a point where it won't show too much. Adjust the position of the dogwood and weave another block of each material (see cover photo).

WALING

Work three rounds of three-rod waling, using no. 8 cane, to make the top of the basket really strong. Tap the waling with a rapping iron to make sure that it is tight and close, and that the side of the basket is the same height all the way round.

ROPE BORDER

This is a very tight border and you will not be able to push the handles through it afterwards without damaging the cane, so if you have not already added liners, do so now.

After damping the stakes well so they are in a good pliable condition for working the border, follow the instructions for the rope border as for the Cheese Tray (but note that in this case there are **double** stakes, so the border will be thicker and a little more tricky to work).

HANDLES

1 Cut two pieces of handle cane about 70cm ($27\frac{1}{2}$in) long. Slype the ends so a long gradual point is formed and then check that they are still exactly the same length.

2 Bend the handle canes gently over your knee to obtain the right curve. Remove a handle liner and push one end down in its place. Take the other end across the basket and down the opposite channel. Do the same with the second piece of handle cane.

WRAPPING THE HANDLES

1 Select and damp ten strands of no. 3 cane, the length of the handle plus 50cm (20in).

2 Slype the ends and insert five into the waling at one end of the first handle bow.

3 Carefully wind them (all together) round the handle bow about five or six times and leave them to rest inside the basket (fig. 107).

Note Be very careful that the canes do not cross over each other, and that they follow the curve of the handle smoothly.

4 Now insert the other set of five into the waling at the opposite end of the bow to the last ones, and wind them back across the bow in the same manner. (They should lie **alongside** the last group of five – see the marked position on fig. 107.) Leave the ends inside.

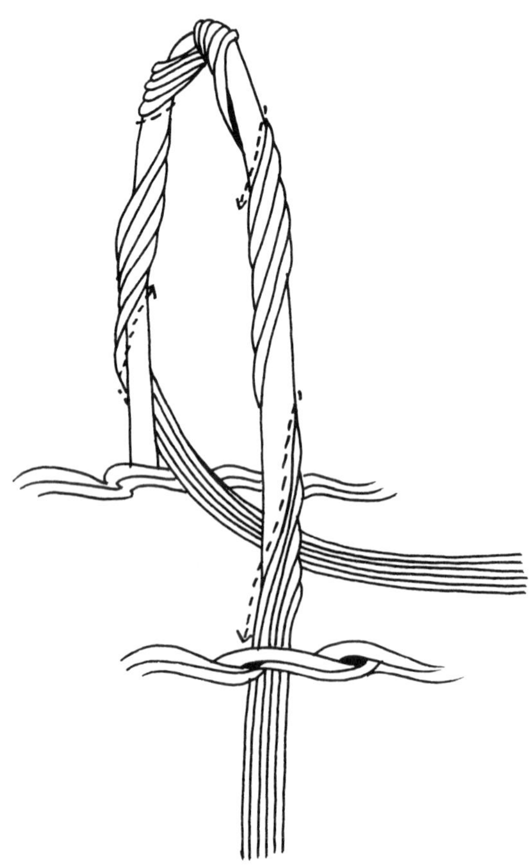

Fig. 107

Fig. 108

5 Now fill the remaining space with additional lengths of no. 3 cane, slyping the ends and pushing them down to the **right** of the groups of five, first one side and then the other, wrapping them in turn, one at a time, and adding new canes until the space is filled.

6 Make sure that the ends are still damp, and if not give them a spray, then thread them all through under the waling to the outside of the basket, on the right of the handle.

7 The ends of the cane must be in the right order and not twisted round each other.

8 Take them one at a time, diagonally across to the left-hand side of the handle, round the back of the handle and back across the front from right to left, threading the ends through under the waling to the inside. Do the same with the rest of the ends (fig. 108).

9 Take the damp ends across and thread them one at a time under the group of canes on the inside (see colour photo). Do not cut them off yet.

10 Repeat steps 6 to 9 with the ends at the other side of the handle.

11 Insert and wrap the second handle in the same way.

12 Finish off all four groups of ends, either as shown in the photograph, or take them through to the outside of the basket under the waling and thread them away in and out as inconspicuously as possible.

WRAPPING THE TWO HANDLES TOGETHER

1 Tie the handles together with two pieces of string just beyond the place where you want the wrapping to start. This will act as a guide for starting and finishing and will also hold the two together. (The string will be removed afterwards so do not wrap over it.)

2 Select a piece of dogwood about 15cm (6in) long. Damp a length of no. 6 cane (long enough to wrap without joining). Turn an end of the cane, about 5cm (2in), at 45°, place this short end under the handles, and start wrapping, catching in the end to cover it.

3 Wrap round the two handles tightly about five times and then slip the piece of dogwood under the turns so that it lies over the handle join. (If the twig is too bulky split it in two, placing the cut end downwards.)

4 Work across the handles, wrapping twice under the dogwood and three times over (see colour photo).

5 When there are about 4cm ($1\frac{1}{2}$in) left to wrap before the string is reached, place a small piece of no. 12 or 14 cane under the handle and wrap tightly over this too. Finish the wrapping to match the start, carefully pull out the short piece of cane and thread the end of the wrapping cane back through the channel created when the short cane was removed.

6 Pull gently but firmly on the end of the wrapping cane while tightening the wraps by twisting with your spare hand!

7 When all is tight and firm, cut off the ends, remove the string. Heave a sigh of satisfaction and stand back and admire your work!

PROJECT 14

Picnic basket with plaited montbretia leaves

Plaited montbretia leaves were used in the side of this basket to add interesting colour and texture. The leaves had been cut the previous year and dried away from the sun so they kept their colour. Any long, strap-like leaves could have been used such as daffodil, rush, reed mace, iris – it is fun to experiment with available materials. Before plaiting, the leaves were damped on the grass with a watering can then wrapped in a damp towel for about an hour to become pliable. I used about 50 leaves which made a plait about six metres (19½ft) long.

MATERIALS

For a basket with a base 33cm × 11cm (13 × 4½in), height 20cm (8in) and top 41cm × 18cm (16 × 7in):

For the base:

- No. 14 cane for the base sticks
- No. 6 cane (two short pieces) for the base
- No. 3 cane for weaving the base

For the side:

- No. 8 cane for the side stakes and top waling
- No. 3 cane for the bye-stakes
- No. 6 cane (natural) for the upsett and chain-waling
- No. 6 dyed (dyed brown) for the slewing
- Six metres (19½ft) of plaited montbretia leaves or other material
- Two lengths of handle cane, 71cm (28in)
- Lapping cane or chair seating cane to wrap handles

Weight of basket 400g (14oz)

PLAITING THE LEAVES

Plait garden materials before starting to make the basket. You can then estimate how many rows can be woven with it and so plan the design of your basket.

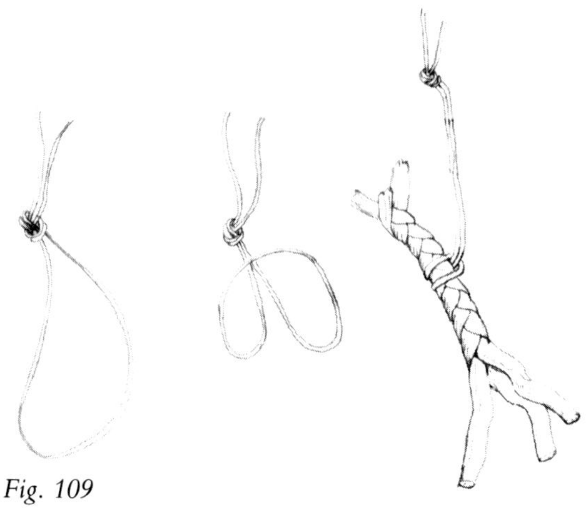

Fig. 109

To plait the material, tie three leaves together with a piece of string and attach the string to something immovable, a table leg for instance. Add leaves as required to keep the plait even.

Note A piece of string tied to a table leg and then looped round the plait will save time tying and untying the plait as it becomes longer and you get further and further away from the table leg (see the cartoon on page 24). Just loosen the tension and pull the newly plaited material through, tighten and continue plaiting (fig. 109).

USING A PLYWOOD BASE

A wooden plywood base with an uneven number of holes drilled at 1.5cm ($\frac{5}{8}$in) intervals could be used. If using this omit the instructions below for making the woven base and start by cutting side stakes from no. 6 cane, 60cm (24in) long.

Follow the instructions on pages 11–13 for staking up with a wooden base and for working a foot trac. Upsett with a three-rod wale for three rows and then continue with the instructions on page 94 (Bye-stakes) for the rest of the basket.

METHOD

1 From no. 14 cane cut five base sticks 38cm (15in) long and 13 sticks 17cm (7in) long.

2 Pierce the short sticks and thread the long ones through.

3 Arrange the sticks (see fig. 103) and wrap with chair cane as in the last project.

4 Slide the short pieces of no. 6 cane in on either side of the wrapped slath (see fig. 103).

5 Soak the base so that the sticks do not crack as they are opened out at each end.

6 With two lengths of no. 3 cane (well dampened) tie in the slath with randing and open out the sticks as in the instructions for the Flower-Gathering Basket.

7 After six rows, start to pull the cane gently and to bend the sticks away from you in order to start crowning the base.

8 Continue to chase round, one row after the other until the base measures about 6cm ($2\frac{1}{2}$in) across. Add another piece of no. 3 cane to each length and slew (see fig. 111 and Note, p. 95) for four or five more rounds, pulling a bit more firmly to continue crowning.

9 Work carefully, pulling just enough to continue shaping. Look at each stick and adjust if necessary to keep each one equally spaced, especially at the rounded ends.

Joining slewing

As in randing (see fig. 39), stagger the joins.

10 If the base has nearly reached the right size 33cm × 11cm (13in × $4\frac{1}{2}$in), take a length of no. 6 cane long enough to go twice round the base with about 20cm over. Damp it and bend it in half.

11 Loop this bend round a stake in the middle of one of the long sides and work a firm row of pairing right round the edge. This finishes the base and gives it a really strong edge.

STAKING UP

1 From no. 8 cane cut 51 stakes 60cm (24in) long.

2 Slype the end of each stake.

3 Soak the side stakes for at least five minutes and push each one firmly down as far as possible into the base, following the diagram of staking up an oval base (see fig. 105).

Fig. 110

Note The odd stake, no. 51, is necessary if you are going to add a length of plaited material without chasing, as in the Doll's Moses Basket.

4 Place the odd stake in the least noticeable position (the widest gap).

5 When all the stakes are firmly in place turn the base right side up (upside-down saucer). Squeeze each stake with a pair of round-nosed pliers and bend up.

Note Bend the first one very carefully. If a crack appears, soak the base and the stakes a little longer until they are really pliable.

6 Tie up the stakes in three groups with elastic bands or string.

THE UPSETT

Mark a stake and work a four-rod pull-down wale (with the basket on its side) using no. 6 cane (see figs. 34–35). Follow this with three or four rows of three-rod waling. This basket should be upsett so the stakes go straight up.

Change the stroke each time you reach the marked stake, and finish correctly as in figs. 10–13 and 15–17.

Note Keep the stakes tied while you upsett the second row. It is a bit tedious pulling the long lengths of cane through, but worth it to keep a good shape. The weavers must be kept damp.

After three rows of the three-rod wale try undoing the elastic bands and see if the stakes are standing up straight. If not, replace the bands and continue with another round, but be sure the upsett does not start to curve inwards. After four rounds of three-rod waling the stakes should be standing up straight. Finish the waling correctly as on pages 19–20. Rap down the upsetting firmly with a rapping iron to make sure there are no gaps between rows.

BYE-STAKES

Either add one no. 6 bye-stake to the right of each stake, or add one no. 3 on either side, making 51 or 102. They should be cut to the height of the finished basket, 20cm (8in), and pointed at one end. Push each one down into the waling beside the stakes, to the right if there is only one or each side if there are two.

SLEWING

'Slewing' is randing with more than one weaver at a time, hence two-rod slewing, three-rod slewing, etc. This weave is useful for helping the work to grow quickly as

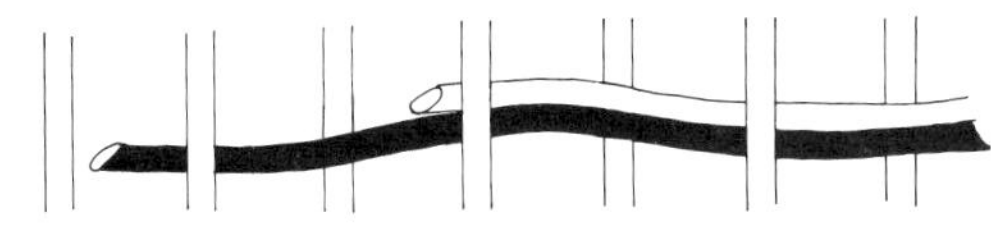

Fig. 111

well as being decorative. In this basket I used a simple two-rod slew (fig. 110).

Pitfall Be careful when slewing not to weave with too many strands of material. The combined strength of the slew should not be stronger than the stakes or it will push them out of shape.

Note If there were an **even** number of stakes it would be necessary to start a second pair of slewing rods when one round of slewing had been completed. These two would chase each other (see page 33).

1 Start one piece of dampened no. 6 cane (dyed brown) in front of one stake and behind the next and then place the second on top of it so the start is staggered (fig. 111).

2 Work with these two together, being careful to keep the stakes upright and evenly spaced. Do not to pull while you are slewing or the stakes will be forced inwards.

3 Slew for 5cm ($1\frac{3}{4}$in) and finish the weaving so there are the same number of rows on each side of the basket.

Joining

Join in new weavers when required. As for randing, stagger these joins and leave all the ends inside.

DOUBLE CHAIN-WALING

'Chain-waling' consists of one row of waling followed by one row of reverse waling which creates the chain. It is used as a decorative or strengthening weave (fig. 112).

This **double** chain-waling uses six thin weavers at a time instead of three thicker ones (see fig. 110). Prepare six long lengths of damp no. 3 cane.

1 Mark a stake, and put the ends of each pair of canes in the next three consecutive spaces to the right.

2 Work the first row of waling, being careful not to twist the pairs that are being woven as one. Keep them side by side.

3 The cane should be damp. Tighten the canes by pulling gently after making each stroke (in front of two stakes and behind one).

Note You will find that it is necessary every four or five strokes to untangle the ends. Hold the six canes about 60cm (2ft) down their length from the basket and

Fig. 112

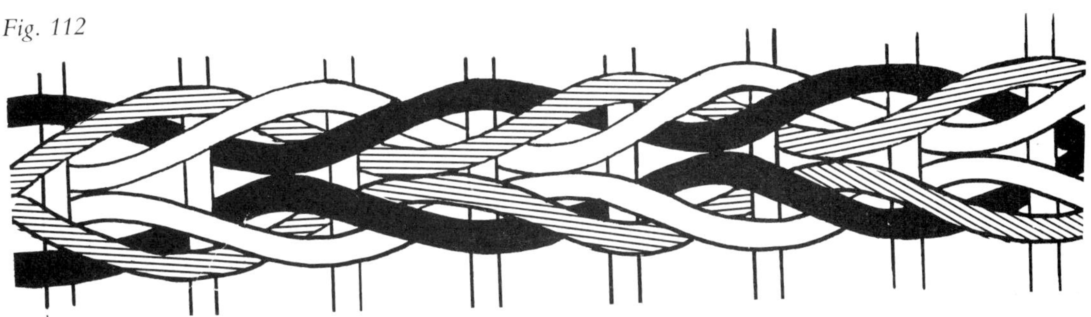

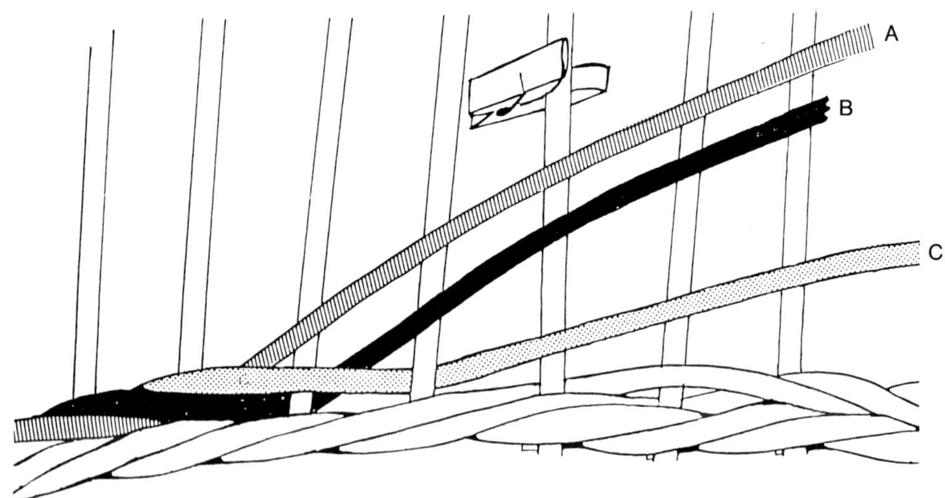

Fig. 113

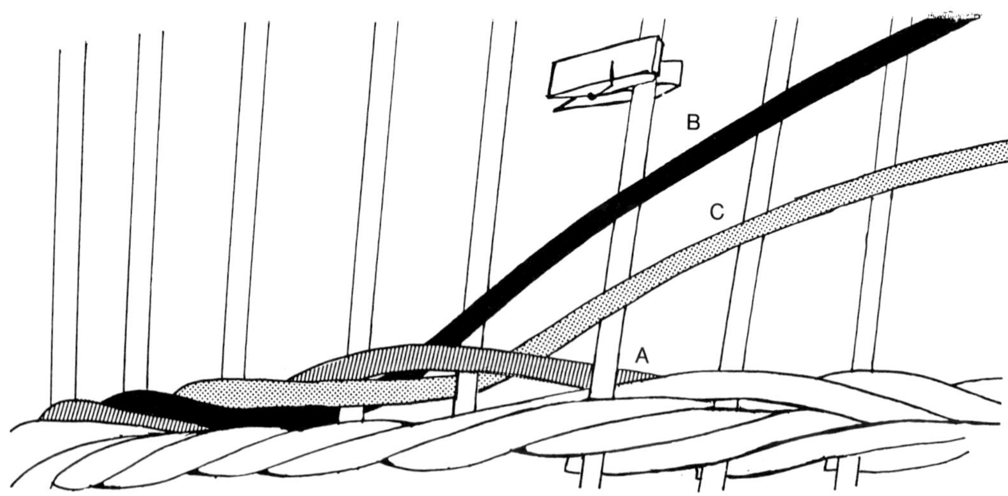

Fig. 114

swing them round in an anti-clockwise direction to untwist the ends, or pull the ends out singly to untangle them.

4 When you reach the left-hand side of the marked stake fig. 113), carefully change the stroke (C, then B, then A – see fig. 114). Then weave a row of reverse waling (see page 95), taking the pair A under B and C, in front of two stakes and behind the third. Watch the shape carefully, pulling slightly on the pairs of canes if you want the basket tightened up and keeping the canes untwisted.

5 Finish correctly following figs. 115–116.

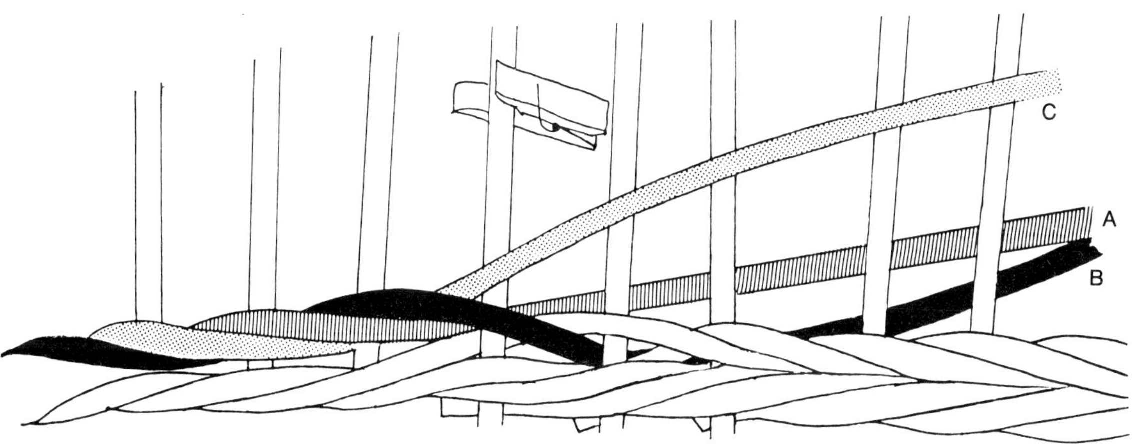

Fig. 115

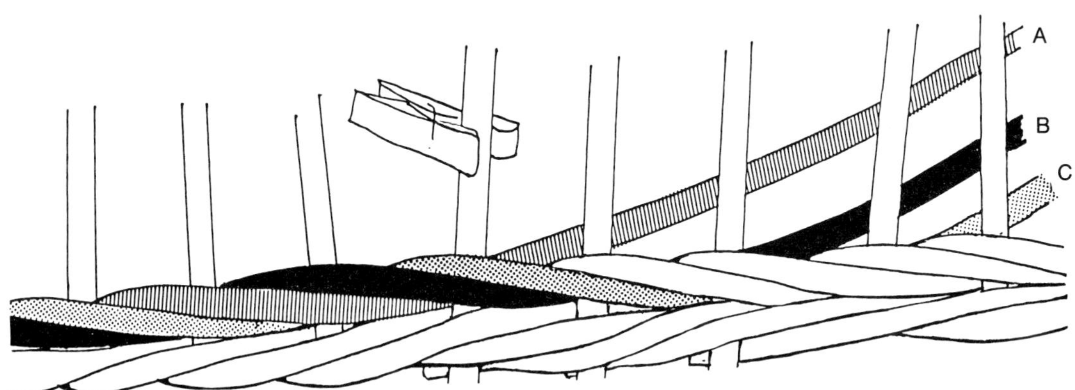

Fig. 116

Joining

Avoid joining if possible by using six full lengths of cane. But if it is necessary, join as in waling (see fig. 14).

Measure the basket to check the height all the way round before continuing with the weaving. Tap down with the rapping iron to adjust the high spots, or compress with fingers if there is only a small adjustment needed. Make sure all the rows of slewing are tight one upon the other.

WEAVING IN THE PLAIT

1 Start at the tapered end where you began the plait and weave in and out of the stakes for about five rows. Take the plait carefully **round** the stakes. Do **not** pull but weave in front and behind, without altering the position of the stakes.

2 Continue until you reach the starting point and have not enough plait left to work another round. Taper the end of the plait by undoing and cutting a few ends. These can be glued later.

DOUBLE CHAIN-WALING

Work another row of chain-waling as above.

SLEWING

Work another band of slewing as before, being careful to keep the shape controlled.

THREE-ROD WALING

Using no. 8 cane (natural) work a strong band of waling to finish off the weaving. Remember to mark the stake to the left of the start. Change the stroke at this point on each row and finish correctly (see figs. 10–13 and 15–17).

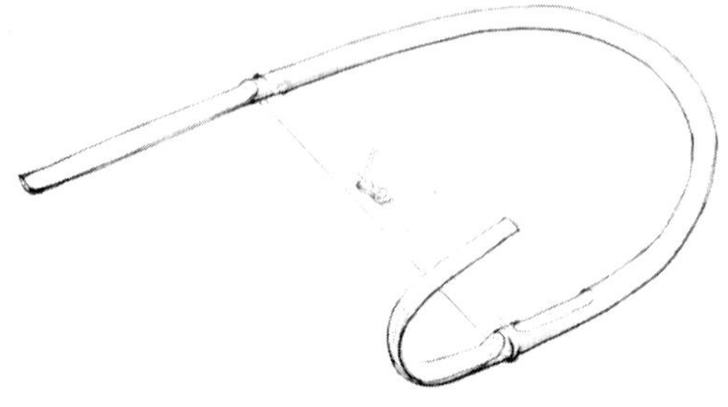

Fig. 117

THREE-ROD PLAIN BORDER

Follow the instructions for a three-rod plain border given on pages 50–53.

FOLLOW-ON TRAC

Follow the instructions on page 54.

HANDLES

The following instructions are for a pair of drop handles to fit over the border. (Alternatively they may be fastened to the sides with a loop of lapping cane – the whole handle and its wrapping being completed before it is attached.)

1 Cut two lengths of handle cane 68cm (27in) long.

2 Carefully carve out and thin down the last 12cm (5in) of each of the four ends.

Note Bend the handle bows to the right shape, tie them and lay them flat on the table. Mark where to cut so the slypes are in the right place (fig. 117).

3 Soak in hot water for about ten minutes and shape the ends round the handle of a bodkin, making sure the curve is smooth.

4 Tie them up until dry.

5 Next day, thread the ends through under the border from the outside. Fasten the ends to the handle on the inside with sellotape and wrap the handles with glossy lapping or chair seating cane.

6 Damp the wrapping cane. Lay the right side of one end of the wrapping cane on the handle bow, pointing upwards. Holding this in place, start wrapping the handle, binding in the loose end at the same time.

After a few wraps insert a short length of the same cane you are wrapping with, this will lie on top of the handle and be wrapped over and under (see the handle wrapping instructions for the Cheese Tray). This extra piece of cane, known as a leader, helps to keep all the wrappings in place as well as being decorative.

7 To finish, wrap to the end of the handle. Then allow the last three or four rounds to slacken, while holding the other rounds tightly above them.

8 Turn the end and thread it up between the slackened rounds and the bow with the right side facing the bow. Tighten again, twisting the wraps of cane and at the same time pulling the end up. A little glue on the end before threading it ensures a firm finish.

9 Fill your basket and go off for a well-deserved picnic!

PROJECT 15

Ali Baba basket

I have had this basket for 30 years. It was a wedding present and has been used for all the family washing ever since. It is still as good as new. By popular demand I am giving a short recipe as the final project of the book.

MATERIALS

For a basket 70cm ($27\frac{1}{2}$ in) high:

- No. 12 cane for stakes
- No. 8 cane for upsetting, for the lid sticks and the three-pair plait round the edge of the lid
- No. 6 cane for randing, slewing, waling and pairing the lid
- No. 3 cane for starting pairing the lid and the five-strand plait handle
- A round wooden base 31cm ($12\frac{1}{4}$in) with 35 holes drilled 2.5cm (1in) apart to take no. 12 cane

Weight of basket approximately 2kg (4lb 8oz)

METHOD

1 Cut 35 stakes from no. 12 cane 81cm (32in) long, and 35 bye-stakes 70cm ($27\frac{1}{2}$in) long.

2 Soak the ends of the stakes in hot water for ten minutes.

3 Stake up the wooden base and work a foot trac.

4 Work three rows of three-rod waling using no. 8 cane.

5 Insert a bye-stake on the right-hand side of each stake.

6 Work 16cm ($6\frac{1}{2}$in) of randing with no. 6 cane.

7 Work two rows of waling.

8 Make a twisted ring from no. 12 cane with a 150cm (59in) circumference, and fix it round the stakes (thread some through the twists) 48cm (19in) up from the base. This will help with guiding the shape.

9 Work 8cm (3in) of slewing.

10 Work two rows of waling.

11 Work 8cm (3in) of randing.

12 Work two rows of waling.

13 Work 9cm ($3\frac{1}{2}$in) of slewing.

14 Remove the ring and work two rows of waling.

Fig. 118

15 Tie the stakes and rand for 14cm ($5\frac{1}{2}$in), bending the stakes in until the circumference is approximately 1m ($39\frac{1}{2}$in).

16 Work two rows of waling.

17 Work 2.5cm (1in) of randing

18 Work two rows of waling.

19 Cut 35 stakes for the border from no. 6 cane 38cm (15in) long. Slype the ends and push well down between the stakes and bye-stakes, to a depth of at least 12cm (8in).

20 Cut off the **bye-stakes** and work another two rounds of waling, weaving straight upwards.

21 Work one more 2.5cm (1in) block of randing.

22 Finish with four rows of waling using no. 8 cane.

23 Cut off any remaining ends from the no. 12 stakes.

24 Work a three-rod plain border with the no. 6 stakes.

THE LID

1 Cut ten sticks from no. 8 cane 36cm (14in) long.

2 Make a slath by piercing five sticks and threading the other five through.

3 Pair round three times and open out.

4 Pair for 4cm ($1\frac{1}{2}$in).

5 Work two rows of waling using no. 6 cane.

6 Add a no. 8 bye-stake 12cm (5in) long beside every stake. Slype one end and push down as far as possible into the pairing.

7 Work follow-on randing with no. 6 cane for 7cm ($2\frac{1}{2}$in).

8 Open out the stakes and bye-stakes with four or five rounds of waling until the lid **just** overlaps the top of the basket.

9 Cut 40 stakes for the plait border from no. 6 cane 36cm (14in) long.

10 Stake up, pushing the ends about 4cm ($1\frac{1}{2}$in) into the edge of the lid. Cut off the ends of the **sticks**.

11 Work a three-pair plait.

12 Weave a five-strand plait for a handle, threading two lengths of cane through the lid (making four strands) and adding one more. (Colour photo shows different handle).

13 Plait, following fig. 118. When the plait is long enough thread the ends to the inside, damp well and fasten with a reef knot. Glue if necessary.

Hedgerow woods

Hedgerow materials can provide a range of beautiful colours which more than make up for any effort involved gathering them.

CUTTING AND PREPARATION

Material is cut in winter, November to March, when the sap is down and the leaves have fallen. Bundle and label the rods according to variety, size and length and leave in a sheltered spot (under a hedge for instance) to begin to dry out a little. 'Clung' (partially dried) material when supple needs no other preparation. This can take as little as two or three weeks. Pithy woods need longer. If the hedgerow material is used before it has shrunk sufficiently the work will become loose as further drying out occurs. Hedgerow 'stuff' (as basketmakers call their working material) remains clung until April when spring warmth dries it still more and it becomes unworkable. Then it might just as well be thrown away.

If the stuff is to be used while the weather is still cold and before it is sufficiently clung, then it may be necessary to bring it indoors for a few days before using. Do not bring it into a centrally heated house, just a shed or garage. If the stuff is allowed to become too dry it will need soaking and there is the possibility of the colour being spoilt.

Make sure the material you gather is not too thick for easy use – nothing thicker than a pencil for medium-sized baskets. Choose fast-growing material such as willows and poplars, as the shoots are inclined to be long in comparison to their width. Most suitable rods are to be found on shrubs or hedges which have been cut the previous year.

Avoid sappy woods such as elderberry and rods with side shoots, unless the side shoots are themselves long and straight enough to be used. Ideally you should try to gather rods about 50cm (20in) to 60cm (24in) long although shorter rods can be used for slewing. Gather 30 rods of each type if possible. If only a few of a kind can be found these can be used to bring attractive colours into the side of a basket, as in the Cane and Willow Bread Basket.

Look for rods which

- are straight
- have no flaws or blemishes
- are of a reasonable length as compared with thickness
- taper from butt to tip
- are pliable enough to bend round your fist
- have attractive bark that stays attractive when dried

- are of one year's growth only (in the second year rods become woody)
- have only a small amount of pith.

SOME SUGGESTED MATERIALS

Willows
Lime suckers
Elm from hedges
Wych-elm
Hazel and ash (for handles)
Poplar (Lombardy)
Cornus (dogwood)
Honeysuckle (wild and cultivated)
Clematis (old man's beard)
Privet
Purging buckthorn
Virginia creeper (hanging variety)
Bullace
Wild lilac
English maple
Snow-berry
Spindle-tree
Bramble (remove thorns)
Dog rose
Periwinkle
Wild plum
Jasmine (summer and winter)
Spiraea
Southernwood (old man or lad's love)
Wayfaring tree
Philadelphus
Larch
Hornbeam
Ivy roots (grow above ground in woods)
Apple prunings

These are just some of the woods that it is possible to use.

When gathering hedgerow material for basketmaking, look for stems that are long and smooth, pliable and of a colour and texture that pleases you. Then try them out! But do remember not to choose rods with butt ends any thicker than a pencil.

Glossary

Base Bottom of the basket.
Border Top edge of a basket.
Brown willow Willow dried with the bark on.
Buff willow Commercial willow which has been boiled and stripped. The tannin in the bark colours the wood.
Building up Weaving backwards and forwards to raise the level of weaving in a particular area.
Butt Thicker end of a willow or hedgerow rod.
Bye-stakes Second stake inserted next to the main stake for extra strength.

Centre cane Also known as pith cane, pulp cane, wicker and reed. From rattan which is imported from the Far East.
Chain pairing. A row of pairing and a row of reverse pairing together forming a chain.
Chain waling A row of three-rod waling and a row of reverse three-rod waling together forming a chain.
Chair cane Shiny split rattan used for chair seating and in basketmaking.
Changing-the-stroke (Also known as the Step-up). Reversing the order of weaving at the end of each row of waling.
Chasing weave Used in randing and slewing where there are an even number of stakes.
Clung Term used in hedgerow basketmaking, meaning material is partially dried out and ready for use.
Cross-over handle Type of handle which crosses over the basket from side to side.
Crowning the base Weaving the base so that it is domed rather than flat.

Double chain waling Chain waling worked with three pairs of weavers instead of three single weavers, for decorative purposes.
Drop handles Handles fixed over the border of a basket which can be folded down.

Feeders Lengths of cane added at the beginning of a plait border.
Flow The outward slope of the side of a basket.
Follow-on-randing See Chasing Weave.
Follow-on-trac Weaving away the ends of a border.
Foot trac (or track) Usually refers to the weave used to secure stakes in a wooden base.
French randing Method of randing used mostly when working with willow or hedgerow to compensate for the material being thicker one end to the other.

Glossy lapping cane Hard glossy outer skin of the rattan, mainly used for wrapping handles.

Handle bow Length of firm material used to form the foundation of a handle.

Handle cane 8mm cane used for handles.

Handle liners Short lengths of cane or willow inserted beside a stake in order to keep a space open for the handle.

Hanging loop A length of cane inserted into the weaving and wound several times round itself to form a loop.

Hedgerow material Material suitable for making baskets gathered from gardens and hedgerows and used while it remains clung.

Lapping cane Similar thickness and use as in glossy lapping cane but without the shiny outer skin.

Leader Length of cane or a rod taken across the top of a handle. Other material is then wrapped over and under it to form a pattern.

Mellow Cane, rush, willow or hedgerow in suitable condition for working.

Opening out the slath Fanning out the base sticks after they have been tied in the middle with two rounds of pairing (tying-in the slath).

Packing See Building Up.

Pairing Two weavers worked in turn forming a twist round each stake. The right hand weaver is taken over the left with each stroke.

Pegging the handle A short piece of slyped cane or willow driven obliquely through the waling handle bow to prevent the handle working loose.

Picking off Trimming loose ends from the finished basket.

Plait border Flat border resembling a plait which can be varied in shape and width.

Pricking up Method used for bending stakes at a right angle without cracking them.

Randing Continuous weaving in front of one upright and behind the next.

Rattan Tropical climbing palm mainly found in the Far East.

Reverse pairing In *reverse* pairing the left hand weaver is taken *under* the right with each stroke.

Rod A shoot of willow or "hedgerow" used in basketmaking. Also known collectively as material or stuff.

Rod border Commonly used border, can be three, four-, five-rod etc. depending on the ultimate width and strength required for the top of the basket.

Rolled border Simple border with several variations, woven in stages, each one complete in itself.

Rope border Border in which the stakes are twisted together giving the appearance of a rope.

Seagrass Twisted cord of natural material sold in skeins.

Singeing Burning off the wispy ends from finished canework.

Slath Base sticks of round or oval basket, crossed over and tied together to form the centre of the base.

Slewing Weaving with more than one length of material at a time. Two-rod slew, three-rod slew etc.

Slype Slanting cut on a rod or stake.

Spiral waling Three-rod wale woven in different colours over a set number of stakes in order to create a spiral pattern.

Stakes Upright canes or rods which form the framework of the side of the basket.

Staking-up Pushing the slyped ends of the side stakes into the base.

Stepping-up Another term for the change-of-stroke.

Sticks Thick canes or rods which form the framework (spokes) of the base.
Stroke The single action of a weaver.
Stuff Material used in basketmaking.
Swing handles Handles bound to the side of a basket which can fold up or down.

Tip (or top) Thin end of a rod.
Trac (or track) Simple weave used in foot trac or border (as in follow-on-trac).
Twist tie Paper covered wires mainly used for securing plastic bags.

Upsetting Term used for the rows of waling at the foot of a basket which set up the stakes at the correct angle.

Waling Weaving consecutively with three or more canes or rods to form a strengthening or decorative weave.
Weaver Refers to the cane or rods used for weaving over and under the stakes and sticks which form the framework of the basket.
White willow Willow rod which has been stripped of bark to expose the white wood.
Wooden base Plywood base with holes drilled at regular intervals to accommodate side stakes.
Woven base Base made entirely of woven material.

Cane sizes

This table shows the sizes of cane to use if you now wish to design your own baskets.

Type of basket	Cane size no.	Max. distance between stakes at the border cm	in
Child's (small)			
Base sticks	8–10		
Side stakes	6–8	2–2.5	$\frac{3}{4}$–1
Weavers	3–5		
Shopping (medium size)			
Base sticks	10–12		
Side stakes	8–10	2–3	$\frac{3}{4}$–$1\frac{1}{4}$
Weavers	5–6		
Shopping (large)			
Base sticks	12–15		
Side stakes	10–12	2.5–4.5	1–$1\frac{3}{4}$
Weavers	6–8		
Linen basket			
Base sticks	15		
Side stakes	12	3–4.5	$1\frac{1}{4}$–$1\frac{3}{4}$
Weavers	6–8		
Log basket			
Base sticks	8mm handle cane		
Side stakes	15	4–6	$1\frac{1}{2}$–$2\frac{1}{4}$
Weavers	6–8		
Miniature work			
Stakes and sticks	1–3	1–1.5	$\frac{3}{8}$–$\frac{5}{8}$
Weavers	000–0		

Further reading

Olivia Elton Barratt, *Basketmaking*, Chas. Letts and Co. Ltd.

Olivia Elton Barratt; *Rushwork*, Dryad Press.

Mary Butcher, *Willow Work*, Dryad Press.

Charles Crampton, *Canework*, Dryad Press.

Sue Gabriel and Sally Goymer, *The Complete Book of Basketry Techniques*, David and Charles.

Jill Goodwin, *A Dyer's Manual*, Pelham Books.

Flo Hoppe, *Wicker Basketry*, Interweave Press, Colorado.

Kay Johnson, *Canework*, Dryad Press.

Barbara Maynard, *Modern Basketry Techniques*, B.T. Batsford.

Thomas Oakey, *The Art of Basketmaking* (obtainable from the Basketmakers Association, see Suppliers).

Helen Richardson, *Fibre Basketmaking*, Kangaroo Press.

Lois Walpole, *Creative Basketmaking*, W. H. Collins.

Dorothy Wright, *Baskets and Basketmaking (The Complete Book of)*, David and Charles.

Field Guide to the Trees and Shrubs of Britain, Readers Digest.

The following books are out of print but may be obtainable from a library.

Germaine Brotherton, *Rush and Leafcraft*, B.T. Batsford.

K. Whitbourn, *Introducing Rushcraft*, B.T. Batsford.

Dorothy Wright, *A Caneworker's Book for the Senior Basketmaker*, Dryad Press.

Suppliers

UK

Dryad, P.O. Box 38, Northgates, Leicester LE1 9BU.
Tel: 0533 510405

Reeves Dryad, 178 Kensington High Street, London.
Tel: 071 937 5370

Fred Aldous, P.O. Box 135, 37 Lever Street, Manchester, M60 1UX.
Tel: 061 236 2477

Frank Herring, 27 Higher West Street, Dorchester, Dorset.
Tel: 0305 267917

Jacob, Young & Westbury, JYW House, Bridge Road, Haywards Heath, Sussex RH16 1TZ.
Tel: 0444 412411

Smit & Co. Ltd., 99 Walnut Tree Close, Guildford, Surrey GU1 4UQ.
Tel: 0483 33113

The Cane Store, 207 Blackstock Road, Highbury Vale, London N5 2LL.
Tel: 071 354 4210 (also supplies commercial willow and rush.)

RUSH SUPPLIERS

Country Chairman, Home Farm, Ardington, Nr. Wantage, Oxon. (English rushes.)

John Excell, The Cane Workshop, The Gospel Hall, Westport Langport, Ilminster, Somerset. (Dutch rush.)

WILLOW SUPPLIERS

P.H. Coate & Son, Meare Green Court, Stoke St. Gregory, Taunton, Somerset.

R. R. Hector, Willow Growers & Merchants, 18 Windmill Hill, North Curry, Taunton, Somerset TA3 6NA.

USA

Allen's Basketworks
8624 SE 13th
P.O. Box 02648
Portland, OR 97202
(503) 238-6384

The Caning Shop
926 Gilman St.
Berkeley, CA 94710
(415) 527-5010
800-544-3373

Carol's Canery
Route 1, Box 48
Palmyra, VA 22963
(804) 589-4001

Connecticut Cane & Reed Co.
P.O. Box 762
Manchester, CT 06040
(203) 646-6586

The Country Seat
Box 24, RD 2
Kempton, PA 19529
(215) 756-6124

English Basketry Willows
RFD 1, Box 124A
South New Berlin, NY 13843-9649
(607) 847-8264

The H.H. Perkins Co.
10 S. Bradley Rd.
Woodbridge, CT 06525
(203) 389-9501

Plymouth Reed and Cane Supply
1200 W. Ann Arbor Rd.
Plymouth, MI 48170
(313) 455-2150

Royalwood, Ltd.
517 Woodville Road
Mansfield, OH 44907
(419) 526-1630

CANADA

Caners Corner
4413 John St.
Niagara Falls
Ontario L2E 1A4
(416) 374-2632

D.L. Reed and Company
153 Colbeck St.
Toronto
Ontario M6S 1V8
(416) 763-1079

W.H. Kilby & Co., Ltd.
1840 Davenport Rd.
Toronto
Ontario M6N 1B7
(416) 656-1065

Great Aunt Victoria's Wicker
Box 133
Waubaushene
Ontario L0K 2C0
(705) 538-2071

Crafter's Haven
121 Ilsley Avenue
Dartmouth
Nova Scotia B3B 1S4
(902) 468-5849

THE BASKETMAKERS' ASSOCIATION

The Basketmakers' Association was formed to help promote the knowledge of basketry and allied crafts, through the provision of courses and workshops. It also helps to assure the continuing supply of materials and tools necessary for the craft.

Membership is open to all who are interested and application forms may be obtained from Olivia Elton Barratt, Millfield Cottage, Little Hadham, Ware, Herts. SG11 2ED.

Index